Building a Church From the Top Down

The Architecture of an Effective Church

Marty Guise
&
Bill Wichman

Copyright © 2003 by Marty Guise & Bill Wichman

Building a Church From the Top Down
by Marty Guise & Bill Wichman

Printed in the United States of America

ISBN 1-594672-32-6

All rights reserved. No part of this publication may be reproduced or transmitted in any form or by any means without written permission of the author.

Unless otherwise indicated, Bible quotations are taken from New International Version (NIV) of the Bible. Copyright © 1985 by Zondervan.

Xulon Press
www.XulonPress.com

Xulon Press books are available in bookstores everywhere, and on the Web at www.XulonPress.com.

Introduction   vii

Is there a Plan B?   11

Tier 1 – Mission   19
   Motivation   21
   Obedience   35
   Vision   51
   Attitude   67

Tier 2 – Unity   81
   Relationships   83
   Communication   99
   Structure   113

Tier 3 – Planning   131
   Objectives   133
   Strategy   151

Tier 4 – Hard Work   167
   Implementation   169

Riding the cycle   183

Introduction

There is nothing quite like the feeling of a nail as it pierces your skin and sinks deeper into flesh. There is a small sharp pain at first, similar to a bee sting or a needle. However, the pain instantly intensifies as the nail penetrates more deeply. The agony is extreme and violent. Everything else vanishes from the mind as you can focus on nothing more than the removal of that nail.

Working on construction sites with my father unfortunately resulted in my experiencing that particular pain several times. It is obviously a problematic location as scraps of wood are scattered about and nails dropped without a second thought. My father's specialty was rehabbing old houses, so the sites were often even worse because of the amount of teardown and removal of old material. Regardless of how careful I was, there always seemed to be at least one nail that found its way into my foot!

The lessons I learned from my father building and repairing homes have often resurfaced as I began working with churches. I've learned how important it is to carefully plan a project with the "homeowners." It is also apparent how important it is to have an effective team that is in agreement with each other. The team must work through an agreed upon strategy and then do a lot of very hard work.

Every Christian has been hired on to work in the kingdom through the vehicle of the church. Our jobs are very different, but each person contributes to the work of building an effective church. The challenge of building an effectively functioning church is immense. The roles of the pastors and lay leaders are key to effectively work the plan. The goal of this book is to provide the architecture of a systematic, Scriptural model to intentionally train and motivate church leaders in the work of the church. Reading through this book and exploring the exercises both individually and as a team will help the reader to understand and embrace the work of the church. It is important and it is necessary.

The premise is this: the work of the church is extremely significant and we must be highly effective in carrying out that work. The ministry for which I have the privilege of working, Lay Renewal Ministries (LRM), has been working with churches for fifty years. That experience has led to a conviction that there are some generic building blocks that each church should have in place to assure effectiveness in ministry. As you explore your way through this book, consider this an environmental blue print to be used to build an architectural design that will assure your effectiveness as a church. It is this blue print and these building blocks that will make up the design that will be dwelt upon throughout this book. This architectural design is simply called The Ten Components of the Effective Church.

While working on homes with my father, I learned many things. Typically within a home undergoing rehab, some things simply need to be removed and totally replaced. Other elements are structurally solid and do not need anything more than touch-up. Of course, there are always some areas with parts that need pieces replaced or new support systems to be restored to good order. If you look at the Ten Components listed and believe you have many or all of them in place, wonderful! Many churches have a few of these components in place – whether intentionally or simply by accident (also known as Divine Design!). Others operate acknowledging each component but do not engage them to their fullest extent. Few churches understand the interdependency and hierarchy of these components. Based upon years of practical experience, LRM believes that this very specific structure provides the basis, or skeleton, for healthy functioning and vitality in the church. With intentionality, churches can scripturally position themselves to profoundly impact the world as they subscribe to these components.

As you observe the architecture, you will quickly realize

that visually, this in not the way to build a house. The inverted pyramid can be troublesome until you realize that in this architectural design, the foundation must be on the top. This is a God-built, top-down architecture. Only as God works through the moving of the Holy Spirit will your church plan be effective. The Church is His instrument. It is His plan.

Please also understand one additional key fact. There are no Lone Rangers in the church. On the construction site, much of the project is actually subcontracted to several other workers or companies. The carpenter is not an expert plumber, nor is the plumber an expert electrician. Each person must work in the areas in which he or she is gifted. If you commit to studying this architectural design and implementing it within your fellowship, consider who among your current and prospective leaders will be able to stand alongside you in your quest to serve the kingdom. A true leadership team will need to work together to develop a common trust and respect for each other – and a common motivation for the task at hand. It really is an awesome job – just watch out for the nails!

Is There A Plan B?

Why me? Is there anyone who has not asked that question? Allowing me to work inside of other people's homes while wielding a hammer certainly caused me to wonder what my father was thinking! I was young and honestly not very good with tools. And yet, for some strange reason, my father thought I could be trusted to use the right amount of nails in the right places to hold a wall in place. Unbelievable!

Are you ready for another remarkable reality? God, in His mysterious wisdom, chose **man** to accomplish His plan on earth! It is beyond our human capacity to understand why the most powerful being in the universe and Creator of ALL things would select man – sinful, fallen and defiant man – to do His bidding.

The mystery only continues to grow as we ponder why God would ordain THE CHURCH as the mechanism through which man is to accomplish His plan. It is enough of a challenge for each individual man and woman to discern and accomplish God's plan for his or her lives. How then, can people with their diverse personalities, multiple agendas, motives and expectations possibly be able to work together? There must be a better way!

There's not.

For all of its shortcomings, problems and mistakes, the church has persevered throughout the centuries. Regardless of the sometimes-limited effectiveness and on-going challenges, it is still God's plan. If you believe that God does not make mistakes (and, by the way, He does not), then the Church is exactly the right tool to accomplish God's plan.

There is no Plan B.

There is hope. In His perfect wisdom, God has ordained that certain members of the church be called out to serve as leaders. He has detailed the criteria and the responsibilities for leadership in His Word. Scripture often uses the directionless wanderings of sheep to exemplify their need for leadership. Human beings also need shepherds. God's people need leaders to guide, nurture, protect and "grow them up." There is no higher calling. As leaders in the church, you must understand that the work is extremely significant, you must be highly effective and it will be totally fulfilling IF you are working according to His plan.

Over 500 years ago, a man had a plan. It was very specific and he was committed to the course. Christopher Columbus was determined to find a way to the Indies without the long journey southward. He had his plan and believed he would be able to change the world forever with a new route.

He failed.

In fact, he was a complete failure. Columbus never found the path he was determined to discover. However, with the benefit of hindsight, we can see that he found something which was much more significant and worthwhile. He discovered a new continent.

When you considered or accepted the call to be a leader in the church, what did you think you would accomplish? When I accepted my first leadership position, I honestly expected to change the face of the church and Christianity in the world. Why not? I could see things that needed to be changed. I could see areas to be improved in our church. I could see ways to reach out to the community. I could see how we could better serve our missionaries.

I failed.

The question is why? Why do so many of us fail as we seek to serve God, through His vehicle, the church? Consider the following axiom:

- God commissioned the Church for the purpose of changing the world.
- He promised us that He would empower us with what is needed to carry out the task.
- For the most part, the Church is not significantly impacting the world today.
- Therefore, we must not be appropriating all of the power that God has promised to us.

Analyzing the reality of this axiom and dealing with its ramifications is the greatest challenge of church leaders today. Never in the history of Christianity has focused, intentional leadership been more important. Christianity is crying out for leadership. How do we better appropriate God's promised power? How can we be more effective?

Leadership Effectiveness Training will be driven by this

axiom. It will be driven to help you impact both your own life and the life of your church, community and the world. I failed because I believed I could do it. It is not something that I could ever do. However, through the power of Christ and the effective appropriation of the power He has promised us, WE can do it.

As we study the blueprints and the architectural design of an effective church, the importance of the underlying structure necessary to insure ongoing health will be apparent. Wise leaders are always mindful of this architectural design and perform evaluations to make sure that the underlying support system of the church continues to be strong and healthy. The most effective structure is always built by a team of unified individuals working with a common plan.

In order to begin to work on the process, it is important to agree on some basic assumptions. One of my favorite construction stories is of the drywaller who rushed through a job without going over the plans thoroughly. The plumber arrived during the job and realized that the walls in which he would need to lay pipe were already finished! It was an expensive way to learn to work together from the beginning.

First of all, we must agree on the word "church." The word church does not appear in the Bible until the writing of the New Testament. Our word "church" comes form the Greek word, "ekklesia," which means "a people called out by God for a special purpose." [Just for the record, that is the only Greek word in this book!] We see it first in Matthew 16:18.

> *And I tell you that you are Peter, and on this rock I will build my church, and the gates of Hades will not overcome it.*

Considering this is the first time the church is made reference in the Bible, that is a pretty strong statement. It is actually a fairly comforting one as well. First of all, He does the building. Our greatest design could not begin to touch on the awesomeness of God's building. He is also protecting us. So strong is His church to become, Hades cannot defeat it.

He does have a plan for the church. He chose each person who is a part of His church for a specific reason and a specific purpose in the church.

> *For we are God's workmanship, created in Christ Jesus to do good works, which God prepared in advance for us to do. (Eph. 2:10)*

God has a specific plan for each church. The purpose statement of the church is clear.

> *Therefore go and make disciples of all nations, baptizing them in the name of the Father and of the Son and of the Holy Spirit. (Matthew 28:19)*

> *He said to them, "Go into all the world and preach the good news to all creation. Whoever believes and is baptized will be saved, but whoever does not believe will be condemned. (Mark 16: 15-16)*

> *But you will receive power when the Holy Spirit comes on you; and you will be my witnesses in Jerusalem, and in all Judea and Samaria, and to the ends of the earth." (Acts 1:8)*

We are to tell the world about who Jesus is in our lives. The church is to help equip disciples. God provides us with a model of the church through His Word in the book of Acts.

> *Those who accepted his message were baptized, and about three thousand were added to their number that day. They devoted themselves to the apostles' teaching and to the fellowship, to the breaking of bread and to prayer. Everyone was filled with awe, and many wonders and miraculous signs were done by the apostles. All the believers were together and they had everything in common. Selling their*

possessions and goods, they gave to anyone as he had need. Every day they continued to meet together in the temple courts. They broke bread in their homes and ate together with glad and sincere hearts, praising God and enjoying the favor of all the people. And the Lord added to their number daily those who were being saved. (Acts 2: 41-47)

We know, without a single doubt, that the early church was vital. Scripture records time and again hundreds and thousands of individuals coming to a saving faith in Jesus Christ as they interacted with the members of that first church.

This is where it gets really interesting. For the most part, the essential disciplines of the modern day church are no different than the disciplines of the first church. There are essential elements of ministry that must be included in our actions as a church. If any of those elements are missing or weak, we will not have the success that was experienced by the first church.

These essential elements include the following:
- Worship
- Prayer
- Relationship Building
- Preaching and Teaching
- Missions / Outreach
- Evangelism
- Stewardship
- Sacraments

This is obviously a generic list. Each church must individually subscribe to its own essential elements. The extent of emphasis on each element however, varies greatly. This is where leadership must be engaged. Leaders must be intentionally seeking and striving to accomplish God's purpose for their specific church.

There is no Plan B.

    Accept it.

        Work with it.

            Thank God for it.

Action Steps:

As you consider the following questions, think about what impact the answer would have on your church today. How would it impact your church tomorrow? In the corporate world, two questions effectively determine the purpose and success of any business:

1. **What's your business?**

What are the things that your church is intentionally seeking to accomplish? What's your mission?

_____
_____
_____
_____

2. **How's business?**

How well are you doing these things?

_____
_____
_____
_____

How do these two questions apply to your church? Do you have an intentional plan as church leaders? How will you accomplish it? The Ten Components of the Effective Church will help you to answer and to act on these questions.

Level 1 – Mission

All authority has been given to Me in heaven and on earth. Go therefore and make disciples of all the nations, baptizing them in the name of the Father and the Son and the Holy Spirit, teaching them to observe all that I commanded you, and lo, I am with you always, even to the end of the age. (NAS)
                                        Matthew 28: 18-20

People need a mission, a purpose for existing. They need to be excited about what they are involved in to be truly successful. (Simply look at the amount of time corporate America spends on encouraging employees through simple posters to extravagant company picnics for proof of this fact.) The healthy church needs to feel confident that it is squarely planted within God's will. When we feel that what we are doing is significant, we are wiling to extend ourselves in working for that cause. Matthew 9:36 states, *"And seeing the multitudes, He felt compassion for them, because they were distressed and downcast like sheep without a shepherd.* When we do not have direction, it is like not having a shepherd. Many churches today are downcast and feel like a sheep without a shepherd. Many pastors today are likewise downcast, feeling like they have lost their sheep. The first step then, is for leaders to understand God's mission for their church.

Four components make up the first and most important level of an effective church. The elements of motivation, obedience, vision and attitude must be the bedrock foundation of the church. They serve together to define the mission with which the members of the church strive to work together to carry out God's will for both their lives and the church.

Let's Party!

⁂

D o you know any "partiers?" I'm sure you know the type. Their day does not start until the sun goes down. Stories of their wild escapades are always related to you through wide-eyed acquaintances who cannot believe what the partiers did this time.

Personally, my favorite "partier" is David. Take a moment to visualize his most famous party moment.

> *So David went down and brought up the ark of God from the house of Obed-Edom to the City of David with rejoicing. When those who were carrying the ark of the Lord had taken six steps, he sacrificed a bull and a fattened calf. David, wearing a linen ephod, danced before the Lord with all his might, while he and the entire house of Israel brought up the ark of the Lord with shouts and the sound of trumpets.* 2nd Samuel 6: 12b-15

If you didn't smile when you read that passage, take a minute to read it again please – and when you do, really put yourself into the passage. Imagine the rejoicing faces all around you. God was returning to the City of David! Imagine the sight of David as he danced WITH ALL HIS MIGHT. Sweat is flying everywhere. Arms are raised in praise. Open your ears to the sound of trumpet blasts and shouts! People are bursting with joy! I hope you are smiling now.

I hate to do this to you, but let's consider the next passage as we learn that Michal, daughter of Saul, is not joining in the celebration.

> *As the ark of the Lord was entering the City of David, Michal daughter of Saul watched from a window. And when she saw King David leaping and dancing before the LORD, she despised him in her heart. ... Michal ...said, "How the king of Israel has distinguished himself today, disrobing in the sight of the slave girls of his servants as any vulgar fellow would."* 2nd Samuel 6:16, 20b

Talk about a splash of cold water on your face. Michal did not join "the entire house of Israel," but rather "watched from a window." David's reply to her is immediate and honest:

> *It was before the LORD, who chose me...I will celebrate before the LORD. I will become even more undignified than this and I will be humiliated in my own eyes.* 2nd Samuel 6: 21b-22a

David's motivation was pure and clear. David's motivation was a joyful celebration, grown out of loving appreciation of his choosing before the Lord. His life became a literal dance before the Lord as he was compelled by the knowledge of the One who gives us life.

As you look at your own <u>church life,</u> is your motivation for serving as a leader more like that of a David or Michal. Are you able to gladly leap and dance for joy when called upon to prepare the budget? To fix a leaky toilet? To visit someone in the hospital?

> *For Christ's love compels us, because we are convinced that One died for all, and therefore all dies. And He died for all, that those who live should no longer live for themselves but for Him who died for them and was raised again. So from now on we regard no one from a worldly point of view. Though we once regarded Christ in this way, we do so not longer. Therefore, if anyone is in Christ, he is a new creation; the old has gone, the new has come! We are therefore Christ's ambassadors, as though God were making his appeal through us. We implore you on Christ's behalf; be reconciled to God.* 2 Corinthians 5: 14-17,20

We are no longer our own. We live not for ourselves, but *for Him who died.* Therefore, our motive is now to live our lives for Him as His ambassadors in the world. WOW! God has specifically chosen you to be His special emissary to accomplish a great work for Him.

He has also promised to empower you to accomplish this task.

In light of this, we must be very careful to guard our motivation. The temptation to allow pride to enter our hearts is constant. Our motivation must be driven by God rather than men. If we do what we want to do to look good before men, our motives are wrong (see Matthew 6:1). Our motive should be to please God rather than man. Consider this early example:

> *In the course of time Cain brought some of the fruits of the soil as an offering to the LORD. But Abel brought fat portions from some of the firstborn of his flock. The LORD looked with favor on Abel and his offering, but on Cain and his offering he did not look with favor. So Cain was very angry, and his face was downcast."* Genesis 4: 3-5

God knows the heart and the motivation. Both Cain and Abel brought offerings to God. Abel's offering was accepted with favor. Cain's offering was not. The difference is that Abel brought his best to God. Our motivation should be to give our best to God in all that we say and do.

Guiding Principle

Pure motives in ministry are grounded in shepherds who do what they do because of an unquenchable love for Christ and who desire only to see the glory of God enhanced and His Kingdom advanced.
Joseph Stowell

The Challenge of Leadership

Leaders in the church are impacted by the component of motivation based on two principles.

1. Proper and true motivation for serving
2. Creating an environment in the church that God can use to motivate others to seek Him and grow in Him

In addressing those two principles, we can ask the following questions.
- Why must we serve God?
- Why is it important that Christians are motivated to service through their churches?
- Who motivates us in our Christian walk?
- What responsibility does the church's leadership have for the motivation of the body of Christ?
- Who is the focus of our motivation?

Moving through a discussion of these questions and then working through the exercises will help both you and the other leaders in your church to first discover and then embrace an attitude of motivation that flows out of loving appreciation for the One who has given all.

Why Must We Serve God?

Every morning you wake up, get out of bed and start the day. Why? Is it to go to work, earn money and support the family? Do you wake up to take care of the children, get them dressed an off to school? Whatever the reason, something drives you to start moving and live.

Consider the simple and Biblical "wake up" call tomorrow morning. Why should you wake up and get out of bed? Two words:

LOVING APPRECIATION

For Him who died should be taped to your alarm clock, bathroom mirror, car dashboard and your desk at work. *He died for all* – you and me – so that we might join our Father in heaven. It is that loving appreciation that drives us to service and sustains us in our efforts.

The fundamental components for the effective church are a pastor, pastoral staff, leadership team and a congregation that are properly motivated to serve the Lord Jesus Christ. It is a community of brothers and sisters in Christ doing what they do through their church based on the same motivation.

Motivation is the cornerstone of healthy church effectiveness. The proper motivation for Christians is a loving appreciation to a loving God. Vital and effective churches do not function if members serve based on obligation or "duty." Healthy churches have leaders and members who would choose to not only save us from our sinfulness, but who would also call us to serve Him through His church. God's grace is a bigger concept than our finite minds are able to fully comprehend. However, as we daily seek to strive to understand the immensity of what God has done for us through Jesus Christ, we can begin to serve Him based on the proper motivation – loving appreciation.

I love the word "epiphany." It's my light bulb word. When I have an epiphany and the light bulb suddenly appears above my head, it is such a wonderful feeling of a quest solved. All Christians have had a time in their lives when God put that light bulb above their head. Whether brought up in the church or drawn into the family later in life, there was a point in time in which the reality of God and His relationship to you became clear. In fact, most of us can think of several times in our lives that God put a new light bulb over our heads as we experienced various spiritually clarifying moments.

Our unfortunate tendency is to become nonchalant about our relationship with God as we progress throughout our lives. We take our spiritual inheritance for granted. We must not. It is important that as you walk with the Lord and grow in your spiritual life that you constantly remind yourself of *Him who died.* God's motivation never changes. We serve God because of what He has done for us.

Why Is It Important That Christians Are Motivated To Service Through Their Churches?

I'm sure you've heard the 80-20 Principle in churches. 80% of the work is done by 20% of the people. Scripture is clear that we are called to be a community of believers. We are brothers and sisters in Christ. Therefore, we are ALL to work together to accomplish His plans. The Christian life cannot be a solitary journey. It is to be a group endeavor.

> *It is He who gave some to be apostles, some to be prophets, some to be evangelists, and some to be pastors and teachers, to prepare God's people for works of service, so that the body of Christ may be built up until we all reach unity in the faith and in the knowledge of the Son of God and become mature, attaining to the whole measure of the fullness of Christ.* Ephesians 4: 11-13

The Bible makes it clear that all Christians have a role in this plan. More specifically, we have all been given gifts that are crucial to the success of the project we call the Church. Church leaders are called to activate and engage His chosen body of believers to make sure that all of the God-given human resources are contributing to the common good based on each believer's specific gifts.

Many business projects have fallen short due to a variety of reasons. Not enough money. Not enough personnel assigned to the task. The deadline is too tight. The wrong systems were used. The list can go on and on. The question for the church is simply this: "Would God give you a job to do and not give you the means to do it?"

The following statement changes the entire paradigm of leadership in the vital local Christian church. It establishes what the church is to be and how leaders are critically responsible for molding local church bodies into powerful tools for God's use. This statement empowers the effective church by challenging leaders to engage God's workforce, the priesthood of believers.

> **God created the Church. He has a plan for each congregation that He calls. The responsibility of church leaders is to discern what that plan is and to discover, develop and deploy the human resources that the congregation has been given. Each church requires the entire body of Christ to be involved to fully accomplish God's plan. By intentionally and vigorously shepherding the Body, Christian leaders will be used by God to activate a church, which will glorify Him as it accomplishes His will.**

As you unpack and digest that thought and consider its components, what are the ramifications for you as a leader and for your leadership team?

Who Motivates Us In Our Christian Walk?

I once attended a worship service in which the guest preacher brought a basketball, a football and a volleyball. Honestly, I could not tell you anything about the message. I simply remember being very excited when I walked out of the church. As I thought about it later, I was impressed with the speaker's ability to motivate the listeners. How then, are we motivated to serve in our Christian walk?

The Holy Spirit motivates believers to Christian service through their church. God uses men as His instruments to help others understand the greatness of His love for us. Motivation then is proactive. As we learn more about God's love and begin to better comprehend it, we act as a response to that love.

Is your church a place that encourages and enhances the work of the Holy Spirit? Is it winsome and holy and active and alive? Is it inviting and different? Is it an environment that causes and outsider to be intrigued with its spiritual essence? Is it clear that there is something different going on there? As we are considering the Components of the Effective Church, we are considering how we might consistently position churches for God's most impactful use of them. Did any of the preceding questions make you wonder about your own church?

It is, of course, the pastor who is primarily responsible as God's conduit for motivating the flock over which he or she is the shepherd. The most effective strategy for motivating people to come to Christ initially and to continue to seek Him is the steadfast preaching and teaching of the Word. As people understand the truths of the Scriptures as interpreted by God's chosen and ordained leaders, they will be motivated to serve Him fully with their lives.

> *Consequently, faith comes from hearing the message, and the message is heard through the word of Christ.* Romans 10:17

What Responsibility Does The Church's Leadership Have For The Motivation Of The Body Of Christ?

Tyranny of the urgent. This often repeated phrase captures the essence of one of the great spiritual crises of the modern age. The pastor's STUDY has become the pastor's OFFICE. Pastors spend much of their time dealing with the tyranny of the urgent issues rather than concentrating on the primary reason for their calling to preach and teach.

People are motivated as they hear and understand the Truth of the Scriptures. It is the Word of God that touches hearts. The primary function of the pastor in the Christian church is to seek and search out the truths of Scripture and then preach and teach the Word. In order that they might fulfill their God given call, we must assure that pastors are allowed to effectively preach and teach. This takes time, focus and intentionality.

For many people, the new currency of the 21st Century has become time. As leaders in the church, we must consider stewardship, not only of funds, but of time as well. If the role of the pastor is to preach and teach, how can the pastoral staff and lay leadership effectively steward the use of time so that the focus of the pastor is not shifted to other matters?

As leaders consider their responsibility to position the church so that God might use it as a tool for His motivation, the issue of time stewardship is crucial. God always gives the church the resources it needs to get His work done. The most valuable resource is not a balanced budget. The most valuable resources are the people. It is the responsibility of the church to create an environment in which God can best motivate and equip His people so that the entire congregation is engaged in the use of their talents and gifts. This is a church that will glorify God and expand His Kingdom.

Who Is The Focus Of Our Motivation?

David Mains, in his book, The Sense of His Presence, clarifies proper focus like this:

> *When the church is functioning at its best, when it is on fire for the Lord, the presence of Christ is the focus of corporate life. In such a church it's not the building of which people are most proud. The pastor isn't the personality whose name dominates all conversations. The denominational program isn't what is pushed most. It is Christ who is the center of interest.*

People will stay properly motivated, as long as the Motivator is consistently before them. In the Church, it is consistently remembering the love of Christ that is our motivation.

Next to the subdivision where I live, developers recently

Building a Church From the Top Down

began building a new subdivision. It is helping me to learn quite a bit more about the building process. They began by clear-cutting all the trees and vegetation in the areas where they would be building. Following that act of destruction, they began leveling off the ground. What has become a fascinating project to watch has now taken an interesting twist – I can no longer see what they are doing! Why not? They have begun blasting underground in order to lay pipe. A siren blast fills the air and moments later, our walls shake.

In your church, what is necessary to capture and build a sense of proper and true motivation? Applying the building lessons to your church raises some interesting questions. Do you need to do some clear-cutting of programs? Is it time to level off some "processes" and systems that have gotten out of control? Do you need to do some work "underground" – working in key areas or with key people to set some necessary things in place to effectively move into the future? Are you ready for the church walls to start shaking?

We are no longer our own. We live not for ourselves, but *for Him who died*. Shake the walls!

Action Steps:

1. Often in churches, we find the leadership knows very little about one another. As an effort to bridge the gap of understanding, write your "clarifying moment" in one paragraph. How did He touch your soul with the reality of His existence? How did you come to know the immensity of the gift that He has given to you through the life, death and resurrection of Jesus Christ? Share these paragraphs with one another at your next leadership meeting.

   _____
   _____
   _____
   _____
   _____
   _____
   _____
   _____
   _____
   _____
   _____
   _____

2. Ask the members of your congregation to write their own one paragraph "clarifying moment." Create a Testimony Journal made up of all the personal moments of your congregation. Make copies of the journal available to members and add new testimonies as new people join your fellowship. (Imagine the size of the book in five years!)

3. Develop a forum to ask your congregation to consider their place in the "Priesthood of Believers." Help them understand that it is no coincidence that God has brought them to your church. Indicate the willingness of the leadership of the church to help

each member discover, develop and deploy their spiritual gifts and talents for the good of the Kingdom.

4. Establish a task force to study the *Tyranny of the Urgent* in your church. Explore how other church members might handle some of those "urgent" things that detract the pastor from preaching and teaching. (Implementing this concept in your congregation will probably require some education with firm ground rules. If the reasons are fully communicated and explained, they will be accepted and your church will be blessed.)

Follow the Boss

T ear down your house. Totally. Flatten it like a pancake and haul off the debris. In its place, I'd like you to build a thirty-story building, forty feet wide and forty feet long. It needs to be built entirely out of metal and glass. Each floor needs to have ten rooms and one bathroom. Sound absurd? Just wait!

Now go down to the local homeless shelter and find two hundred and ninety-nine families to move into the building (you can take the last room). Make sure you stop by the grocery store because you will need to feed everyone for the next year. I'm going to lock the doors from the outside so you won't be able to leave.

Will you do it? Somehow I doubt it. I certainly wouldn't do it if someone asked me to do it. You would have to be crazy to even attempt something that ludicrous.

Remember a guy named Noah? He had a little visit from God. God told him some pretty unbelievable things. Once again, imagine the setting. Picture yourself standing next to Noah and his family as they labor to build the massive ark and complete the task.

> *I am going to put an end to all people, for the earth is filled with violence because of them. I am surely going to destroy both them and the earth. So make yourself an ark of cypress wood...But I will establish my covenant with you, and you will enter the ark – you and your sons and your wife and your sons' wives with you. You are to bring into the ark two of all living creatures, male and female to keep them alive with you.* Genesis 6: 13-14a, 18

Would you have picked up a hammer to help? If I had been Noah's friend, I would have looked at checking him into an institution. Noah had a different reaction. *Noah did everything just as God commanded him.* (Genesis 6:22) **That, my friends, is obedience.**

So what makes Noah so special? Out of everyone living on the entire earth, how could he be the only person who was considered righteous? Noah had the strength of character to be able to build a huge ark on dry land. Can you imagine being his neighbor?

My neighbor built a fence and, in my opinion, destroyed a picture perfect setting of green space. I was ready to go through the roof, but I didn't have anything to complain about compared with Noah's neighbors! Why did he do it?

Let's allow the writer of Hebrews to shed some light.

> *By faith Noah, when warned about things not yet seen, in holy fear built an ark to save his family. By his faith he condemned the world and became heir of the righteousness that comes by faith.* Hebrews 11: 7

Noah obeyed because he had faith. It is that simple. Noah had faith enough to obey God and act – even though, to ordinary eyes, he had lost his mind.

> *Through Him and for His name's sake, we received grace and apostleship to call people from among all the Gentiles to the obedience that comes from faith. And you also are among those who are called to belong to Jesus Christ.* Romans 1: 5-6

Obedience comes from faith. God's grace and apostleship is bestowed upon us so that we are able to call non-believers to the obedience that originates from faith. We belong to Jesus. What does that really mean?

> *Remain in Me and I will remain in you. No branch can bear fruit by itself; it must remain in the vine. Neither can you bear fruit unless you remain in Me. I am the vine; you are the branches. If a man remains in Me and I in him, he will bear much fruit; apart from me you can do nothing. If anyone does not remain in me, he is like a branch that is thrown away and withers; such branches are picked up, thrown into the fire and burned. If you remain in me and my words remain in you, ask whatever you wish, and it will be given you. This is to My Father's glory,*

that you bear much fruit, showing yourselves to be My disciples. As the Father has loved Me, so I have loved you. Now remain in My love. If you obey My commands, you will remain in My love, just as I have obeyed My Father's commands and remain in His love. John 15: 4-10

This key passage is crucial when considering the importance of our responsibility in church effectiveness. We obey God out of faith. Faith is strengthened as we remain close to that source of power. The only way we can continue to appropriate that power is to stay connected to the power source. If we stay connected by abiding in Him, there is nothing that we cannot accomplish. We will be very effective for the Kingdom. The message is very simple.

But the one who hears my words and does not put them into practice is like a man who built a house on the ground without a foundation. The moment the torrent struck the house, it collapsed and its destruction was complete. Luke 6: 49

Our effectiveness must be built on the firm foundation of our faith in and obedience to Jesus Christ. Obedience follows faith. Effectiveness follows obedience. Are you ready to build that house now?

Guiding Principle
True knowledge of God is born out of obedience.
John Calvin

The Challenge of Leadership

Logic would say that the more we learn about God, the more we will be willing to be obedient. Calvin's statement presumes just the opposite. The more we seek to be obedient, the more knowledgeable we will become. The key then, is to understand the concept of dutiful obedience to God in the light of His mercy and grace. If we are to respond to God in loving appreciation, what are the dimensions of an appropriately obedient response?

Leaders in the church are impacted by the component of obedience based on these two principles:

1. Leaders must help people to understand that as Christians, we have been called to live lives very different from the world.
2. Christians must understand what it means to live an obedient life in Christ.

In addressing those two principles, we must ask the following questions:

- What does it mean to be obedient to the calling of Christ?
- How can we best assure our obedience to Christ?
- How will we abide in Jesus Christ?
- How can we best position ourselves to be used for His best purposes?

Moving through a discussion of these questions and then working through the exercises will help both you and the other leaders in your church to explore the power of obedience born of faith.

What Does It Mean To Be Obedient To The Calling Of Christ?

I still remember the first time my son didn't respond to "Because daddy said so." It started out simply enough. We were cleaning up at the end of the day and I told him to help with a certain task. His question of "Why, daddy?" didn't surprise me. Questions are par for the course with young children. (I once read a statistic that stated children ask an average of 439 questions each day!) Being a semi-normal father, I gave the standard answer of "Because I said so." He very politely replied, "Yes daddy, but why?"

Have you ever asked God, "Yes daddy, but why?" I must confess I have on several occasions. Just as the foundation of love has been laid in my home, the foundation of loving appreciation must be laid in the church. Upon that foundation, obedience rests. John Mac Arthur once said:

> *To understand and to affirmatively respond to the truth of the Gospel of Jesus Christ is to have one's time and eternity completely altered.*

Faith in Jesus causes us to respond with **loving appreciation**. True obedience is a natural outgrowth of Godly motivation. Obedience is a function of true faith. If we have even an elementary understanding of the extent of His love for us and in turn we seek to respond to Him in love, we will have an inbred desire to be obedient to His calling on our lives.

It really is exciting to think about this calling of obedience. After being called by God to follow Him, you passionately want to respond out of sheer appreciation. That response of appreciation drives you to determine exactly what course He has planned for you. Scripture states it plainly.

> *I know, O Lord, that a man's life is not his own; it is not for man to direct his steps.* Jeremiah 10: 23

> *In his heart a man plans his course, but the LORD determines his steps.* Proverbs 16:9

So what does it mean to be a leader in the church? Or rather, how does obedience manifest itself in leadership? The New Testament supplies us with a thorough list of leadership criteria. Understanding this list helps us to discern the first reality of leadership criteria. The Scriptural qualifications Paul presents through the Holy Spirit in 1st Timothy and Titus 1 are these:

> We are to be:
> Blameless, hospitable, lovers of goodness, self-controlled, upright, holy, self-disciplined, holding to the Word as taught, able to give instruction in sound doctrine, able to refute those who would oppose doctrine, above reproach, with good reputation, respectable, able to teach, gentle, good managers of our households, raisers of believing children, sincere, tested first, faithful, full of the Spirit and wise.
>
> We are not to be:
> Overbearing, quick-tempered, violent, greedy for gain, quarrelsome, lovers of money, recent converts or addicted to much wine.

To put it simply, these lists are humbling. Bill Hull, in his book, <u>Building High Commitment in a Low Commitment World</u>, boldly summarizes the criteria appointing church leadership: "An obedient church is one that appoints leaders who are gifted and spiritually suited for the task – anything less is sin."

A Godly leader understands that based one's own qualifications, he or she is totally unworthy to serve as God's instrument. Therefore, they must be constantly seeking His power, wisdom and strength in order to be effective. He is the potter and we are the clay.

How Can We Best Assure Our Obedience To Christ?

To best answer that question, I will once again appeal to the inspired writer of Hebrews.

> *Therefore, holy brothers, who share in the heavenly calling, fix your thoughts on Jesus, the apostle and high priest in whom we confess.* Hebrews 3:1

The first step in the Christian walk is repentance. This message of repentance has been trumpeted since the fall of man in the Garden. God will not use us if we are not able to first acknowledge our sinfulness, realize our inadequacies and lean on Him for our empowerment. Only the repentant heart can be used by God.

> *For the grace of God that brings salvation has appeared to all men. It teaches us to say "No" to ungodliness, worldly passions, and to live self-controlled, upright and godly lives in this present age, while we wait for the blessed hope – the glorious appearing of our great God and Savior, Jesus Christ, who gave Himself for us to redeem us from all wickedness and to purify for Himself a people that are His very own, eager to do what is good.* Titus 2: 11-14

Obedience to Christ can only be assured through Christ. Have you ever gone swimming in a cold pool? The only way to really get in is to just jump in and totally immerse yourself in the water. Your body temperature quickly adjusts to the cold and in a few minutes, you don't even realize how cold it initially felt.

In the walk of Christian faith, we must jump in and totally immerse ourselves in the waters of Christ. It is this depth of abiding in Him that guides our course and helps us to be leaders at home, at work and in the church.

How Will We Abide In Jesus Christ?

One of the greatest challenges of the Christian life is understanding what it is that God requires of us. What specifically is Christ calling us to do as we respond to him? We are saved by grace, but what is our responsibility beyond accepting our salvation? Does our part end there? As God chose us, what were His intentions for us? This question has been a wrestling point for both theologians and lay people. The theologians of the seventeenth century approached this question and responded to it through the Westminster Confession of Faith.

The third question of the Shorter Catechism and its answer are as follows:

> Question 3: What do the Scriptures principally teach? The Scriptures principally teach, what man is to believe concerning God, and what duty God requires of man.

Even the Reformers recognized that God's gift of grace to us was not to stand in isolation. There must be some spiritual response from us. So just how are we to determine the appropriate level of response?

We must first understand that our obedience cannot be based on our attempt in any way to repay Christ based on what He has done for us. Human obedience is fully unsatisfactory. There is no amount of sacrifice or devotion that even approaches sufficiency when we consider the enormity of what God has done for us. Mankind cannot repay God for His gift of redemption through Jesus Christ.

Does this mean that we then succumb to our ineptitude, rationalizing that there is nothing that we can do to pay Him back? Therefore, any effort on our part is meaningless and there is no use in committing any part of our lives to Him? That is obviously irrational thinking also.

Consider the early church and the disciples that were closest to Jesus Christ physically and spiritually. These were the men that knew Him best. We must consider their willingness to commit their lives to Him. Nearly all of those early followers literally gave their lives for Him. Their obedience was inspired. Their obedience was total. Consider this example from Paul:

Are they servants of Christ? (I am out of my mind to talk like this.) I am more. I have worked much harder, been in prison more frequently, been flogged more severely, and been exposed to death again and again. Five times I received from the Jews the forty lashes minus one. Three times I was beaten with rods, once I was stoned, three times I was shipwrecked, I spent a night and a day in the open sea, I have been constantly on the move. I have been in danger from rivers, in danger from bandits, in danger from my own countrymen, in danger from Gentiles; in danger in the city, in danger in the country, in danger at sea; and in danger from false brothers. I have labored and toiled and have often gone without sleep; I have known hunger and thirst and have often gone without food; I have been cold and naked. Besides everything else, I face daily the pressures of my concern for all the churches. 2 Corinthians 11: 23-28

Is this the kind of sacrifice and suffering that Christ expects of us today? Can any of us say that we have experienced even a small amount of persecution equivalent to that which Paul endured for the sake of the cross? How then can we know what obedience means for us? In John 15, which we discussed earlier, Jesus called for us to abide in Him. God initially motivates us to love and serve Him through His church. This one time activation is not enough. As we abide in Christ, we "stay attached" to God so that He can continue to work on us and through us. The dictionary definition for abide is as follows:

Abide: to stand fast; remain; go on being. (Webster's New World Dictionary)

There is an implication of consistency and perseverance in that definition. So "abiding in Christ" implies that we must seek ways to assure an ongoing connection with Him. There must be a constant attachment so that we can continue to draw strength from the Source.

As you continue to reflect on what it means to abide in Christ, use the following principles as a method to enhance your spiritual walk. They will help us to abide in Christ. This path of obedience has served as a formula for devoted followers of Jesus throughout the centuries.

PRINCIPLE ONE:
In order to position ourselves so that we are ready, willing and able to accomplish God's plan for our lives, we must be seeking to become more Christ-like. The more obedient we are to God's calling to godliness, the more effective we will be in His use.

How can we expect our ministry through our churches to be blessed and impactful, if we do not have a vibrant, consistent relationship with God? Effective church leaders are in constant touch with God. To understand this in detail, we move to Principle number two.

PRINCIPLE TWO:
The most straightforward path to godliness is to understand the spiritual disciplines and to consistently live a more spiritually disciplined life.

If there is to be any "striving" in our quest to be more obedient either as Christians or as Christian leaders, our striving should be **towards godliness**, not towards being better Christians or better Christian leaders. There is a difference.

This quest toward Christ-likeness can be accomplished as we seek to be more disciplined Christians. Donald Whitney describes spiritual discipline as follows in his book, <u>Spiritual Disciplines for the Christian Life</u>:

The Spiritual Disciplines are those personal and corporate disciplines that promote spiritual growth. They are the habits of devotion and experiential Christianity that have been practiced by the people of God since Biblical times. The Spiritual Disciplines are the God-given means we are to use in the Spirit-filled pursuit of Godliness.

The Spiritual Disciplines as described in Whitney's list are as follows:
- Bible intake:
  - Hearing the Word
  - Reading the Word
  - Memorizing the Word
  - Meditating on the Word
- Prayer
- Worship
- Evangelism
- Serving
- Stewardship
- Fasting
- Silence and Solitude
- Learning
- Journaling

(There are several other books on the Spiritual Disciplines with slightly different lists depending on the experience and attitude of the author. Another book worth recommending is Richard Foster's <u>Celebration of Discipline</u>.)

It is no coincidence that this list includes most of the things to which the 1st Century church devoted itself. To modern, busy Christians, a list this all-encompassing can be overwhelming. In the 21st Century, the pace of life is much more frantic. How can we be expected to spend more time becoming more spiritually disciplined? If we devote ourselves to spending more time to become more spiritually mature, He will multiple our time. This is a spiritual phenomenon that is logically incomprehensible but practically true.

PRINCIPLE THREE:
Spiritual Discipline in the pursuit of Godliness is accomplishable! God would not call us to endeavors

that are beyond our scope of doing. (But we must rely on His help.)

We don't need to understand this principle. We just need to believe it. As Christians – and more importantly, as Christian leaders – our first and foremost responsibility is to seek to be more Christ-like. As we make time to grow closer to Him, He will give us the time to accomplish the things that are important to Him. We must take steps toward our growth. We do not grow in every discipline at once, but He will call us to focus on specific disciplines at specific times in our lives.

As a parent, I have had this fact illustrated for me daily through my children. From the first smile, to the first step, to the first word, to the first day of school, I see my children progressing in life. Life is a journey of steps. As Christians, we just need to be willing to walk with our Father.

How Can We Position Ourselves To Be Best Used For His Purposes?

As we are seeking to abide in Christ, He will use us as instruments of His kingdom. In His sovereignty, God will position us to be used as He directs our path. This is one of the remarkable and hard to believe truths of our faith. Our responsibility is not the "work of the church." <u>Our responsibility is to walk in a manner worthy of His calling</u>. As we seek Him and grow in Him, we are positioned for His use. Spiritual discipline molds us and sculpts us into effective vessels.

The simple truth is that the great leaders of Christendom never strove to be great Christian leaders. They were devoted to growing closer to God. God then used them as great leaders because they had positioned themselves for His greatest use. They were plugged into His power. Billy Graham was once asked, "If you had to live your life over again, what would you do differently?" His response?

One of my great regrets is that I have not studied enough. I wish I had studied more and preached less. People have pressured me into speaking to groups when I should have been studying and preparing. Donald Barnhouse said that if he knew the Lord was coming in three years, he would spend two of them studying and one preaching. (As quoted in Christianity Today, September 12, 1977)

Paul admonishes us:

Therefore, I urge you, brothers, in view of God's mercy, to offer your bodies as living sacrifices, holy and pleasing to God – this is your spiritual act of worship. Do not conform any longer to the pattern of this world, but be transformed by the renewing of your mind. Then you will be able to test and approve what God's will is – His good, pleasing and perfect will. Romans 12: 1-2

This passage summarizes the essence of spiritual obedience.
- We are to offer our bodies obediently to God as living sacrifices.
- We are not to conform to the pattern of this world.
- We are to be transformed by the renewing of our minds.
- Then we will be able to know God's will for us.

In effective churches, people are obedient to God's calling. They understand that in order to be used by God, they must continually be mindful that He is the source of true power and effectiveness. They know that to take advantage of that power they must stay attached to the vine.

If you remain in me and my words remain in you, ask whatever you wish, and it will be given to you. John 15: 7

Action Steps:
1. Growth is vital in our walk with the Lord.
    a. Take some time to do a personal spiritual inventory of your walk with the Lord over the last 12 months. In which areas of your life have you grown in your obedience to the Lord? In which of the areas of spiritual discipline do you feel the most comfortable?

    _____
    _____
    _____
    _____

    b. Again, considering the list of spiritual disciplines, in which areas do you believe you need more work? How is God prompting you right now to commit more intentionally to one or more of these disciplines?

    _____
    _____
    _____
    _____

2. Schedule some time in both your leadership meetings and as a church to conduct some specific teaching and perhaps a pulpit series on repentance and God's grace. Plan a special service devoted to nothing but repentance, praise and worship for God's mercy. Offer a time for individuals to repent of their individual sinfulness and for congregational sins of omission and commission. This type of cleansing and celebration will be both pleasing to God and refreshing to your Body of Believers.

3. Form small groups to study the topic of Spiritual Disciplines. Donald Whitney's book, <u>Spiritual Disciplines for the Christian Faith</u>, is an excellent basis for this course. (Companion study guide is available.)

4. Encourage your leadership and small groups to consider

accountability as a major dynamic of their existence. We all need someone to hold us accountable and the depth of relationship and intimacy in small groups provides a perfect forum for healthy Christian accountability. As we encourage and challenge one another in our Christian walk, we will all grow closer to God.

Finding the Blueprint

Have you ever thought about your dream job? What would it look like? What would the hours be? Benefits? Then again, maybe you already have the best job you can imagine. How about this – would you consider waiting tables for the rest of your life?

For a tremendous example of a visionary, we can turn to a waiter – or to be more precise, a cupbearer. What's that? In Old Testament times, the cupbearer was the person to whom the king looked when he wanted something to drink. While not being exactly the most difficult job in the world, many believe the cupbearer had an additional duty as the taste-tester. Before the king would take a drink, the cupbearer would take a sip. If he did not die, the king knew it would be safe to drink from the cup. The cupbearer would therefore be a very special person to the king and would hold a high degree of trust.

Although the Bible mentions more than one cupbearer, the one that most are familiar with is Nehemiah. Tucked away at the end of chapter one in the book of Nehemiah is the brief statement:

I was cupbearer to the king. Nehemiah 1:11c

How did the man who was a cupbearer become the leader who was chiefly responsible for coordinating the effort to rebuild the walls of Jerusalem in only fifty-two days? He was a man of God who believed in prayer. (It would be wonderful to spend the rest of this book simply looking at this man's life and actions, but that is not our focus. Try reading <u>Visioneering</u> by Andy Stanley for a more in depth look.) Let's take a look behind the scenes.

Hanani, one of my brothers, came from Judah with some other men, and I questioned them about the Jewish remnant that survived the exile, and also about Jerusalem. They said to me, "Those who survived the exile and are back in the province are in great trouble and disgrace. The wall of Jerusalem is broken down, and its gates have been burned with fire. When I heard these things, I sat down and wept.

For some days I mourned and fasted and prayed before the God of heaven. Nehemiah 1: 2-4

Although there is not sufficient time to digress into great detail regarding the walls, suffice it to say that without them, the Israelites were hardly a people. They were defenseless and open to bullying from all those around them. Nehemiah understood the implications immediately and was so torn by it that he could only sit, weep and pray for several days.

Of course, after this he leaped into action, called in the army and the king's personal construction crew. OK – maybe not. What did he do? He continued to pray and seek God's guidance for helping the people in Jerusalem. FOUR MONTHS LATER, he had the opportunity to plead his case before the king. When that opportunity came, he was ready to act (after another quick arrow prayer to heaven!)

Nehemiah understood there was a problem (v. 2-3). Nehemiah was motivated to do something about the problem (v. 4). Nehemiah reached out in obedience to the ultimate Source of help for a solution to the problem (v. 4-11). Nehemiah then received a vision from God for rebuilding the walls around Jerusalem.

I am going to have to ask you to grant me a little latitude at this point. How can I say with such confidence that God gave Nehemiah a vision when Scripture does not explicitly tell us this? I think it was a God-given vision because of the response that Nehemiah received from the king, the subsequent response from the people of Jerusalem and the ultimate success of the project. Given the enormity of the task and the impossible odds, success was impossible unless God's hand was upon the project.

When seeking to build or rebuild the framework of any church, we must likewise feel confident in God's hand upon the church and the plans we are making. A vision from God will be revealed. The vision must be birthed from a motivation of loving appreciation to the Creator and Redeemer. The vision must be prepared out of obedience to the calling of God upon a particular church. The vision with God's hand upon it will succeed even in the feeblest of hands simply because He wills it to succeed.

Where there is no vision, the people perish; but he that keepeth the law, happy is he. Proverbs 29: 18 (KJV)

Sacrificial commitment to a cause requires clear focus as to the intent of the cause. We must believe that what we are doing is significant if we are going to become fully involved.

After this, the word of the LORD came to Abram in a vision: "Do not be afraid, Abram. I am your shield, your very great reward." Genesis 15: 1

God provides the vision and the means to carry it out.

Paul and his companions traveled throughout the region of Phrygia and Galatia, having been kept by the Holy Spirit from preaching the word in the province of Asia. When they came to the border of Mysia, they tried to enter Bithynia, but the Spirit of Jesus would not allow them to. So they passed by Mysia and went down to Troas. During the night Paul had a vision of a man of Macedonia standing and begging him, "Come over to Macedonia and help us." After Paul had seen the vision, we got ready at once to leave for Macedonia, concluding that God had called us to preach the gospel to them. Acts 16: 6-10

As we continue to focus our attention on God, He will keep our vision on track. He plants the seed, waters the seed and helps the seed to grow. We just need to make sure we are attached to the vine and praying to the vinedresser.

Guiding Principle
Vision for ministry is a clear mental image of a preferable future imparted by God to His chosen servants and is based upon an accurate understanding of God, self and circumstances.
George Barna

The Challenge of Leadership

Leaders in the church are obviously greatly impacted by the component of vision. *Braveheart* is one of my personal favorite movies. A turning point in the movie occurs when Mel Gibson turns around the deserting troops with a bold, impassioned speech. The men are called to action and probable death not out of duty, but rather a vision of what their lives will be like if they do NOT fight. A good vision will likewise become a powerful engine that influences everything that the church does. Effective churches must have a clear vision for ministry.

It is first necessary that we define and differentiate the meanings behind words like purpose, mission, vision, objectives and strategies. After we define those words for the purpose of this study, we will then look at the following key questions.

- What is our mission as Christians?
- What is God's purpose for __THE__ Church?
- Why is a specific vision important for each individual church?
- What are the benefits of a vision statement?
- What is the role of church leadership in determining God's vision for our church?
- What are the five vital dimensions of planning?

Exploring the answers to these questions and then working through the exercises will help both you and the other leaders in your church to determine your church's vision by understanding where you are, who you are and who God is.

What's The Difference?

There are many definitions to describe these terms. There are no right or wrong definitions, but it is important that your leadership team comes to consensus as to your church's understanding of the definition of the terms. Everyone must be on the same page regarding your unique understanding of the concepts. For the sake of clarity here, we will define the key terms as follows:

- **Mission**: We define mission as the broad concept of God's plan for your church. In the architecture that makes up the *Ten Components of the Effective Church,* it is mission that lays the Godly foundation that is the top level of our inverted pyramid. Mission includes motivation, obedience, vision and attitude. It is the spiritual environment and the under-girding of all that you do as a church.
- **Purpose**: Determining your purpose as a church prompts your church to answer the question, "Why do we exist?"
- **Vision**: God's vision for your church lays out what you believe God is calling you to be in the future. Every church will have a different vision for why they exist depending on their specific circumstances. The unique vision of your church is determined by the uniqueness of the people of your individual church. The "Divine Design" of each individual serves to make up the total personality of the church.
- **Objectives**: Once you have ascertained what God's vision is for your church, establish objectives or "action areas," which prioritize "how" you believe you are going to accomplish your vision. These are short term and long term. Your objectives translate your abstract ideas into concrete plans. Another definition of objectives is "goals."
- **Strategies**: Once you have established your objectives (or goals), you must begin to lay out the plan that specifically states how you are going to accomplish those objectives. Strategies include specific detail as you document clearly defined and measurable plans. The establishment of time lines will serve to help you determine the pace of your actions.

What Is Our Mission As Christians?

The broad definition of mission for Christians is simply to live the Christian life. We are to be Christ-like. Since we have been motivated by the love of Christ and we have been adopted as children of our Heavenly Father, we are to be obedient to His calling in our lives. Our lives as believers are to be different than the lives of non-believers. Christianity is not simply a concept of what we are. It is an all-encompassing model of what we are to be. We are to be living lives in a manner worthy of our calling. Obviously, the specifics of what this means will be broken down for each individual Christian as he or she determines their own purpose and vision and sets their own specifics objectives and strategies.

What Is God's Purpose For The Church?

"Why are we here?" is a crucial question that must be asked and answered on an ongoing basis. In the corporate world, the development of purpose statements became a highly emphasized endeavor in the nineties. The concept was a very valid one. If those working in the organization understood their purpose as part of something larger than themselves, they would be encouraged to extend themselves for their own betterment as well as that of those around them. "Present thinking" became intertwined with "future thinking."

Similarly, the church has recognized the value of having a purpose statement for the same reasons. The difference in the case of the church is that it is not necessary to create a purpose statement! Jesus himself determined the purpose for the church:

Go and make disciples of all nations. Matthew 28:19a

Every church that is true to their calling as the Body of Christ should embrace Christ's commission as the basis for their own specific purpose statement. **If making disciples is not your basic reason for existence as a church, then you are not accomplishing the main task set out for you as a church.**

A purpose statement, when created for your specific church,

will give your people a rallying call. When asked, they should be able to succinctly state your purpose. It should be easy to remember and recite. Below are some examples of actual purpose statements.

To evangelize, edify, equip and exalt.

To know Him and to make Him known.

To reach the lost, teach the found and make disciples of the Lord Jesus Christ.

To save the lost and strengthen the saved to live bold and courageous lives of Christian witness before a non-believing world.

To worship God, disciple believers, build community within the church, pray for direction, forgiveness and power, and extend compassion to the needy.

Can you see the uniting theme in all of these good purpose statements? "To make disciples"

Why Is Vision Important For Individual Churches?
Successful churches have a clear understanding of God's vision for them. Not the vision of the pastor or the strategic planning committee or the denomination, but God's vision for the church captured through significant amounts of study, prayer and counsel. The vision drives the church to action. The vision becomes the filter through which all church activities are evaluated. Activities that coincide with the vision are pursued, and those that fall outside the parameters of the vision are rejected. <u>Successful Churches,</u> George Barna

It is impossible to embrace a common vision and engage in its accomplishments if that vision is not universally understood and promoted. The downfall of many churches is mixed agendas and expectations as to what the church is trying to be about. Church effectiveness is dependent on all the members of the church working toward the accomplishment of the same agendas. These agendas must be bathed in prayer as the Holy Spirit washes over them. Vision statements clarify a more specific God-given direction for the church. Consider these actual vision statements and see if you can describe the churches that they represent.

> *To attract families by developing an extensive, excellent program of spiritual and relational opportunities for children and youth. The church will focus on family issues as a means to facilitate spiritual wholeness.*

> *To reach out to the greater metropolitan area toward raising up four new churches by 2000, to demonstrate God's love, creativity and power by caring for people working in cooperation with other ministries to reach the region for Christ.*

> *To equip professionals in New York City to impact their web of relationships, focusing on reaching non-Christians through cell groups and market place ministries that address urban needs.*

What Are The Benefits Of A Vision Statement?

Without vision, the motivation and obedience of your people will have no practical outlet. A shared vision becomes the driving force of your church. It assures commonality of purpose. Time and again, churches that have lost vision or failed to communicate that vision have lost members or closed their doors. It is easy to see a church in maintenance mode because its members are lethargic about their roles and unwilling to serve. In his book, <u>The Master's Plan for Making Disciples</u>, Win Arn lists the following benefits of vision statements:

- Unify the members of the church
- Provide motivation for action
- Establish a basis for accountability
- Give assurance that you are doing God's work, not busy work
- Give the church an overall direction
- Define what the church does and does not do
- Alleviate false guilt and provide a basis for measuring accomplishments

After reading over that list, can you not see the difficulties of not having AND not communicating a vision? To further state the need for vision, read this quote from Bill Hull.

The church operates at low efficiency because too few work. Everything the church needs resides in the undisciplined body members, but neglectful leaders have not provided the vision. So much is not done by so many who could do it. Well over 50% of the average congregation is a ministry wasteland. People go unchallenged and untrained, unused and unfulfilled.
<u>The Disciple Making Church</u>

What Is The Role Of Church Leadership In Determining God's Vision For The Church?

First and foremost, it is the responsibility of the senior pastor to champion God's vision for His church. The pastor must be passionately attached to the vision of the church if it is to capture the attention of the congregation.

However, it is very appropriate for the entire leadership team to explore the possibilities of God's vision for the church. The vision should be birthed out of prayer, diligence and commitment to God.

Vision is from God. God has a very specific plan for each local church. God has provided your church with visionary leaders. Your pastor may believe that he has been called as a visionary leader in your church. However, according to a recent George Barna survey, the vast majority of pastors do not consider visionary leadership to be their primary spiritual attribute. If this is the case, the necessity of the leadership team to work together to ascertain God's vision for your church is even more apparent.

What Are The Five Vital Dimensions Of Planning?

There are five vital dimensions that church leaders must understand when they begin to work through a vision casting and master planning process. Churches operate differently than any other gathering of people. We are a community that is to operate with a different set of rules than those used by the secular world. Intentionally taking advantage of the benefits of working within our unique church environments will make the planning easier and more effective. The five dimensions are as follows:

- **Prayer:** The church has been given a mighty tool to discern God's will and accomplish His purposes. If we forego the spiritual resource that has been given to us through the power of prayer, we eliminate our greatest advantage in working together as the community of God.
- **Biblical Prospective:** There is no reason for Christians to struggle with setting up procedures and bylaws. We have already been given a spiritual set of bylaws and a standard of procedures (Structure). In the pages of the Bible, God has exemplified any situation threat we might face and any decision that we might have to make. Master planning

must be accomplished based on a Biblical prospective. All considerations and plans in the church should be weighted according to God's dealings with man as depicted in the Bible.
- **Dialogue:** Talk! It is critical that much time be given to discussing the issues that will impact the entire membership of the church. The way that we go about communicating with one another will greatly impact our success. God has called us to be unified in thought and spirit. As we respect others more than ourselves, we will operate with great effectiveness.
- **Ownership:** As members of your congregation are offered the opportunity to become a part of the planning process, they will support it. Again – the church is a body. All of the parts are important and necessary to healthy functioning of the body as a whole (surveys or town hall meetings). Including all the members of the congregation in the process will help them to own and take responsibility for implementing God's vision.
- **Consensus:** Support for plans and actions should be derived through consensus building, rather than elections. When votes are taken, there are winners and losers. When people are lovingly convinced as to the benefit and spiritual directive of our plans, they will wholeheartedly commit to them. Our main objective is unity in thought rather than division of opinions.

The Importance Of Casting Vision

Early in His ministry on earth, Jesus was standing by Lake Gennesaret teaching the people. Because of the size of the crowd, He climbed into Simon Peter's boat and taught from there. When He had finished speaking, He did something very interesting. He told Simon to go fishing again. Not only did He tell Simon to go fishing, Jesus told him that he was going to catch something.

> *"Put out into deep water, and let down the nets for a catch." Simon answered, "Master, we've worked hard all night and haven't caught anything. But because you say so, I will let down the nets. When they had done so, they caught such a large number of fish that their nets began to break. So they signaled their partners in the other boat to come and help them, and they came and filled both boats so full that they began to sink.* Luke 5: 4-7

Obviously, Simon didn't think going fishing was such a great idea. After all, they worked all night and then they listened to Jesus teach. But Simon follows the command because he recognized the authority and vision of the One speaking to him. They reaped a great reward. And what happened next?

> *When Simon Peter saw this, he fell at Jesus' knees and said, "Go away from me, Lord; I am a sinful man!" For he and all his companions were astonished at the catch of fish they had taken, and so were James and John, the sons of Zebedee, Simon's partners. Then Jesus said to Simon, "Don't be afraid; from now on you will catch men." So they pulled their boats up on shore, left everything and followed Him.* Luke 5: 8-11

No exercise that you undertake in your church is more important than taking the time to discern God's vision for your church, communicating that vision and getting on with accomplishing it.

Action Steps:
1. Vision casting is a process. It is a process that will have a major impact on your church for many years into the future. Needless to say, it cannot be accomplished through a short exercise. However, use these small steps to begin thinking and praying about the vision process. Remember the definition of vision as stated by George Barna: "A clear mental image of a preferable future imparted by God to His chosen servants, and based upon an accurate understanding of God, self and circumstances."
   a. Spend some personal time in prayer for clarity from God as to the future vision of your church. Write down a few of the specific elements that might be a part of your church's future vision.

   _____
   _____
   _____
   _____

   b. Form groups of 4 to 8 people and pray corporately for clarity from God as to the future vision of your church. As a group, take another 10 to 15 minutes to develop a list of specific elements that might be a part of your church's future vision.

2. Schedule a time of praying and fasting for your entire church to seek God's direction for your church. (Make sure you take time to study and teach the Scriptural dynamics of prayer and fasting prior to scheduling the event.) Help your congregation to understand that developing a master plan will be of critical importance to the effective future of your church. Pray for unity and enthusiasm as God reveals His vision for your church to your pastor and leaders.

3. Develop a plan to develop a plan. Begin an intentional process as a leadership team to set the course for your church's future. Taking the time to get an accurate under-

standing of your congregation's current perceptions about your present ministry effectiveness is an excellent starting point.

Lay Renewal Ministries offers two additional tools that will be very beneficial in the vision casting process.

Interactive Master Planning
LRM has also developed a tool to be used by your leadership team and congregation that will walk you step by step through the master planning process. Most churches understand that master planning is beneficial. Many however, do not know how to get it done. Interactive Master Planning (IMP) will provide you with a proven methodology. IMP is delivered using Leader Manuals, Action Plan Workbooks for all key participants in the process and a Power Point Presentation (or overhead transparencies). These tools will introduce and engage your participants in the process.

Church Impact Analysis
It is critical that you have a very clear understanding about the perceptions of your congregation regarding where your church is today. In their minds, how effective are you in accomplishing ministry? Having a good handle on this information is necessary before you can make plans as to where you are going and how you are going to get there. The use of a good survey tool will plot your current situation as seen through the eyes of your membership. LRM employs a tools we call a Church Impact Analysis (CIA). The CIA offers you the choice of two comprehensive congregational surveys followed by an on-site consultation weekend, which will allow you to clearly understand and evaluate your current situation as perceived by your congregation. A key to planning is ownership. A survey tool will bring your people on board and help them to feel part of the process.

The Right Face

"**W**e're going to kill you." "No, come to think of it, if we did that, you would just be dead. How about if we just sell you into slavery. That way, we'll get some money and you will suffer before you eventually die." Hard to imagine, isn't it?

You are probably already thinking about Joseph. He is one of my favorite characters in Scripture. Charting the roller coaster of highs and lows in his life is a guaranteed way of helping someone think that maybe their own life isn't so bad after all!

Let's see: his self-important attitude and preferential treatment had frustrated them to the point of not speaking to him.

> *When his brothers saw that their father loved him more than any of them, they hated him and could not speak to him.* Genesis 37: 4

They finally decided to act after his second dream.

> *"Here comes that dreamer!" they said to each other. "Come now, let's kill him and throw him into one of these cisterns and say that a ferocious animal devoured him. Then we'll see what comes of his dreams."* Genesis 37: 19-20

Deciding that wouldn't be proper or profitable, they then decided to sell him into slavery. Jumping ahead in his life, Joseph was actually blessed in his time of slavery so that he was promoted to the second in command. His master's wife attempted to seduce him, but he stayed true to God and his earthly master. She lies to get revenge and Joseph gets thrown into jail. AGAIN, God blesses him so that the prison warden put Joseph in charge of all that was done in the prison.

> *The warden paid no attention to anything under Joseph's care, because the LORD was with Joseph and gave him success in whatever he did.* Genesis 39:23

In prison, he interprets two dreams for a baker and a cupbearer (!), but is forgotten about by the cupbearer when he was released from prison. Personally, I would have been tempted to give up at that point if I had been Joseph, but God is faithful to him. The cupbearer points the Pharaoh to Joseph to interpret a dream and Joseph becomes number two in the entire kingdom of Egypt.

Several years later, the opportunity for revenge presents itself. His family comes to Egypt to get food during the famine and Joseph can punish his brothers for the suffering they caused him. What does he do instead? He takes care of everyone and provides them with more than they could have imagined. In one of the most powerful passages of forgiveness in Scripture, he tells his brothers after the death of his father, Jacob:

Don't be afraid. Am I in the place of God? You intended to harm me, but God intended it for good to accomplish what is now being done, the saving of many lives. Genesis 50: 19-20

God first, self second. Every time I read that passage, I am amazed at the true enormity of that statement. A death threat, slavery, jail, forgotten about and then he comes back with "Hey, it's ok! God had a plan!" Would you have had the same attitude?

As brothers and sisters, we recognize that we are actually the chosen co-heirs of the Kingdom of God. Our attitudes and the way we live our lives should present to others that we are eternally influenced. Scripture is very clear about the appropriate state of mind for those under the influence of the Holy Spirit.

But the fruit of the Spirit is love, joy, peace, patience, kindness, goodness, faithfulness, gentleness and self-control. Against such things there is no law. Galatians 5: 22-23

Our attitudes both in church and out of church should reflect God's call on our lives to live as if we are God's and to relate to one another differently as brothers and sisters in Christ. Isolationists are not allowed in church! We are called to support and encourage one another. The walk of a Christian is a journey as part of a joy-filled community.

> *Rejoice in the Lord always. I will say it again: Rejoice! Let your gentleness be evident to all. The Lord is near.* Philippians 4: 4-5

The Lord will support us in our attitude of joy. As we stay close to Him, our joy will be complete.

> *To Him who is able to keep you from falling and to present you before His glorious presence without fault and with great joy – to the only God our Savior be glory, majesty, power and authority, through Jesus Christ our Lord, before all ages, now and forevermore! Amen.* Jude 1: 24-25

In the end, it is God that provides us with the attitude that is pleasing to Him, as we surrender our will to Him. It is a process of daily surrender and release. If we simply let His radiance be reflected through us, our countenance will be pleasing to Him. As a result, it will make a difference to those around us as well – both those we are serving with and those whom we are serving.

Guiding Principle

I believe the single most significant decision I can make on a day-to-day basis is my choice of attitude. Attitude is that one thing that keeps me going or cripples my progress. It alone fuels my fire or assaults my hope.
Charles Swindoll

The Challenge of Leadership

If leaders are not outwardly energized and enthusiastic by what God is presently doing and what He **could** be doing through the church, there is little chance that the membership will want to be involved in the work of the church.

Attitude is the catalyst that generates action. Sports teams spend hours upon hours building up team morale and motivation to defeat the upcoming opposition. Teams often put gag orders on players to prevent them from saying anything that might be used as fuel to spark the energy of their foes. The right "speech" given by the coach at half-time can propel a team to victory or allow it to slide into defeat. Victory is the only option.

As God's chosen leaders in the church, you are the coaches to rally your team to effectiveness. Your attitudes will be reflected in the faces of your followers. If you are not excited, why would you expect anyone else to be?

We will look at five key questions while addressing the component of attitude.

- Why is attitude a crucial part of the mission of the church?
- How is the attitude in highly effective churches different?
- What is the frame of mind of Christ-like leaders in the successful church?
- How do we "take-on" the appropriate leadership attitude?
- How much difference does attitude make as we chart the future course of our church?

Why Is Attitude A Crucial Part Of The Mission Of The Church Today?

Joseph is a humbling figure to the receptive heart. How can we look at his life, what he endured and then have the audacity to complain? A God-focused attitude is an incredible thing to observe. Attitude is the fourth building block in the architectural foundation of effective churches. This component completes the underlying level of mission. Let's step back and revisit for a moment the bigger picture of what we are trying to accomplish in the study of the Ten Components of the Effective Church.

The Ten Components are a bigger picture. They are a mind-set. They are a philosophy of ministry. They are the model of the environment that will help you to "do church" the way God intended it to be done. If fully understood and in place for the church to flourish, the work of the church WILL be more effectively accomplished.

If then, the Ten Components are a mind-set, then it is an easy transfer to understand the importance of attitude as a foundational part of that mind-set. As the last foundational building block attitude is the thrust of power to the other three blocks. Motivation flowing from loving appreciation for God's mercy inspires us to service. As God motivates the church, it becomes more obedient to Him. Obedience grows from motivation as the spiritual disciplines deepen in maturity of the faith. Vision operates out of that obedience as we begin to see what God is calling us to do through Him. An expectant, high-energy attitude is the resulting outpouring of that providence within the congregation.

My father-in-law works for a grocery wholesaler. Occasionally, he will receive a product sample that he passes along to my family. I just tried a piece of a new energy-boosting gum. It is actually very hard to type now because my hands are shaking slightly, my heart is racing and I feel like running around. Obviously, this is simply a temporary change in my attitude that will (hopefully) quickly fade. This is not what we want in the church.

Attitude is everything is a saying fully applicable in the life of the church. Human beings require encouragement and stimulation on a day-to-day basis. We want our endeavors to be extremely significant and highly effective. Time is too valuable to waste on what we perceive to be ineffective or futile exercises.

For maximum impact, attitude must be genuine. We don't have to drum up artificial excitement about the importance of a God-given mission because there is no more important endeavor. We are doing God's work. We are His instruments for a lost and dying world. What could be more important? This attitudinal mind set needs to be activated, reinforced and continually nurtured. A high level of spiritual energy in the church will be self-fulfilling. We are God's work force. That is exciting!

How Is The Attitude In Highly Effective Churches Different?

Several years ago, George Barna, the foremost student of churches in America, did an exhaustive study of the church to determine what differentiates highly successful churches from the rest. According to his studies, attitude was a very important component of church success. A summary of his findings is as follows:

> *In successful churches, while the basic elements of their ministry were simple, the diligence with which they pursued excellence in the performance of those basics was instructive. They were not content to get a difficult job done. They strove to do it superbly. The churches maintained that they could always be doing their work more effectively, more efficiently and more extensively. They were convinced that Christ had singled them out to do an important and unique job.*
> *Their attitudes were different:*
> - *They were excited about ministry.*
> - *They were passionate about outreach.*
> - *They entered into their ministry full of expectancy.*

The truth and impact of this finding cannot be over emphasized. Success is contagious. Nothing will grow you ministry, enhance your outreach, strengthen you financial health and maximize your spiritual impact more than people who are obviously excited about what God is doing through your church. Successful churches give off an aura of energy. It is clear to all who visit that something special is alive and moving in successful churches. The reality is that the "something special" is the work of the Holy Spirit. But the outward manifestation of His work is projected through the attitudes of the congregation members. People in successful churches have a visible attitude of expectancy.

What does a parent do when their child brings home an indiscernible painting from preschool? What should a parent do when their child receives a positive grade on a school project on which they have labored? What should a parent do when their child makes the team on a sport? When a child does their best on a test, what should a parent do? Cheer! It is the responsibility of every parent to encourage their children and praise them when they have accomplished a goal or done their best.

Leaders in successful churches are intentional cheerleaders. Their goal is to encourage and to build up the Body at every opportunity. For this enthusiasm to be genuine, leaders need to believe in God's vision for the church themselves. When considering the spiritual attributes of future leaders, attitude should be a major consideration. Do not start to build your house with those who will only tear it down.

What Is The Frame Of Mind Of Christ-like Leaders In Successful Churches?

Successful churches embrace attitudes worthy of an all-powerful God who has entrusted them with His perfect plan. Remember, success is not measured by the world's standards of numeric and financial prowess. Rather, in the church it is measured by the conformity of a church to the plan of God. The dimensions of a Christ-like attitude that encourage success therefore include:

- Energy
- Excitement
- Excellence
- Enthusiasm
- Encouragement
- Expectation
- Empowerment

When God gives us our vision – and we know it is truly from God – there is an **energy** released that cannot be explained. We embrace the reality that we have been given an assignment from the Almighty Sovereign God who assures us that we cannot fail as we progress in His will.

This energy will stimulate an **excitement** as we seek to serve Him and accomplish His purposes. A God-produced energy will bubble up excitement that will carry throughout the entire congregation.

As children of God, there is only one goal that should impact our desire to serve Him. All that we do should be done with **excellence**. All that we do is to give glory to God.

We need to intentionally attack our mission with an **enthusiasm** that is contagious. We are embarking on a journey that will overwhelm us with its success if we hold the course and do our best.

There must be a constant attitude of **encouragement** as we accomplish our mission. An empowered church is a tremendous threat to Satan. He will do everything in His power to discourage and wreak havoc on our plan.

We need to reflect a great **expectancy** as to what God is about to do in our presence. A God with no limitations has commissioned us to labor in His service. Only our own timidity and lack of faith will limit our success.

All of this needs to be under-girded with the knowledge that we have the **empowerment** of the greatest force in the universe. There is nothing that He cannot accomplish. He has promised to do it through us.

How Do We "Take-On" The Appropriate Leadership Attitude?

Attitude is a choice. It is that simple. We allow our circumstances to rule us or we rule our circumstances. God has mandated attitudinal concepts that we appropriate. We are to "rejoice always." We are to "put on" the full armor of God. We are to "renew our minds." As children of God, we are new beings and our inheritance calls us to respond to life in a new manner. We are to live in a manner worthy of His calling.

One of the dimensions of our Christian walk is joy. James puts it thusly:

> *Consider it pure joy, my brothers, whenever you face trials of many kinds, because you know that the testing of your faith develops perseverance. Perseverance must finish its work so that you may be mature and complete, not lacking anything.* James 1: 2-4

The word "it" is very interesting. What did James mean when he used that simple two-letter word? I would simply state "it" means "life." Consider LIFE pure joy whenever trouble comes your way. Not if, but when trouble comes. We are to be joyful in all circumstances. We have a choice. We can choose to be joyful or we can choose to not be joyful. However, God tells us which one we should pick. This is the same phenomenon that we face concerning our attitudes as leaders in the church. We must intentionally take on the dimensions of appropriate attitude as described in the previous section.

Leadership attitudes will have a monumental impact on the attitudes of the congregation and in turn this will directly affect the success of the church. If only one change is caused because of your exposure to this book, that change needs to be an intentional uplift of your own attitude and that of your leadership team. This change alone will have a tremendous impact on your church.

How Much Difference Does Attitude Make As We Chart The Future Course Of The Church?

It is really a simple question. As a leader, do you believe that your church has a future? If it does have a future, do you believe it will be a positive one? Ken Callahan states it this way:

The watershed question for many people in many congregations is: Do we believe that our best years are behind us, or do we believe that our best years are before us. Either way, it becomes a self-fulfilling prophecy.

Twelve Keys to an Effective Church
Kennon Callahan

Teachers are taught and re-taught the concept of self-fulfilling prophecy. If a child is presented with the attitude from the parents or teacher that he or she is a failure, the child normally will become that which is expected. Therefore, the teacher's role (in addition to teaching), becomes one in which they must create an atmosphere of success for each and every child.

Similarly, leaders must also convey an attitude and build that atmosphere of success. The vitality and growth of the local church is critically linked to the congregation's attitude about its future. If church leaders can genuinely send the message that God has great plans for the future and that nothing can stand in the way of those plans, the congregation will excitedly accept the news and invest their lives and families in that future. Positive momentum grows healthy churches.

It should be obvious that presenting a gloom and doom, imminent disaster characterization of the church's future will only lead others into a like-minded downward spiral of hopelessness. Individuals and families will leave to find somewhere they can invest themselves in a positive future. Negative momentum is as powerful as positive momentum.

In churches that are in trouble, the most significant concerns typically become budget focused. In the successful church, the focus must always be evangelistic.

The challenge to healthy churches is to work hard to sustain the positive momentum. This requires frequently revisiting the dimensions that caused health and prosperity in the first place. We believe that those dimensions are embodied in the Ten Components of the Effective Church.

The challenge for struggling churches is to stop the downward spiral, to refocus on God's mission, to rebuild relationships and to do the things necessary to recreate a church that is pleasing to God. **What is the culture that currently controls your church's environment?**

Action Steps:

1. Attitude is key to the future of your church. In light of the previous chapter, it is appropriate to take a few minutes to do a quick evaluation and examination. What can you personally do to improve your own attitude, that of your leadership team and that of your church?

   **Excited – 5 Hopeful – 4 Ambivalent – 3 Worried – 2
   Pessimistic – 1**

   a. Personal Attitude Quotient: Based on the above scale, what is your attitude right now about the future of your church?
   b. Leadership Team quotient: In your personal opinion, what is the attitude of your leadership team right now about the future of your church?
   c. Church Attitude Quotient: In your personal opinion, what is the attitude of your congregation right now about the future of the church?

2. Have the leadership team of your church take the same preceding quick examination. Take the scores of the leaders, and average them together. How are you doing as a team? What can you do to improve that score?

3. Use the Attitude Quotient with the entire congregation. What sorts of results were presented on a personal, leadership and church-wide level? Develop an action plan to determine what you can do in the next few days, weeks and months to grow and encourage new attitudes in your congregation.

4. Begin a series of sermons or lessons to send the message to your church that God anoints the work of the church. To be a part of God's perfect plan is the most exciting and significant function that we can accomplish as human beings. The church will prevail if all of its parts are working in harmony and unity to do God's work.

Level 2 - Unity

Finally, be strong in the Lord, and in His mighty power. Put on the full armor of God so that you can take your stand against the devil's schemes. For our struggle is not against flesh and blood, but against the rulers, against the authorities, against the powers of this dark world and against the spiritual forces of evil in the heavenly realms.
                                             Ephesians 6: 10-12

A church with a firm foundation in understanding God's Mission and its components is a church with tremendous potential. That potential can be short circuited unless the leadership recognizes the importance of the next level or platform of our architecture: Unity. No matter how great a church's potential, a church that is not intentionally seeking to foster and build unity cannot succeed. At this level the architecture takes on a new spiritual dimension. The challenge of effectiveness now requires the acknowledgment of spiritual warfare.

Christ knew full well that our biggest obstacle as brothers and sister in the family of God would be the challenge of unity. In His high priestly prayer recorded in John 17, Jesus asks God for one thing for His chosen, called out people – ***perfection in unity***. The church will only be successful to the extent that it can become unified behind its mission. Unity must be a daily goal. A unified church will accomplish much for the Lord. Without such togetherness, our effectiveness will be nullified.

The level of unity consists of three components: Relationships, Communication and Structure. An effective church is one that can begin with a foundation of mission and work together. Effective Unity is defined through three components: relationships, communication and structure. A church failing to function with unity will forgo the completion of its mission.

Teamwork Under Christ

Sitting in El Salvador on a patio chair overlooking the Pacific Ocean while the gentle ocean breezes gently drifted in, my friend remarked to me as we sipped lemonade, "This is what we call *Suffering for Jesus.*" I laughed so hard I almost fell out of my chair. It wasn't that his statement was particularly funny. It just came at the end of an unusually difficult week of working with a team and doing some very grueling physical labor. Twenty-four hours previous, this scene would have been unimaginable. However, we had just taken the team back to the airport for their return home and we were on our way back to clean up. This brief roadside respite was not on my agenda, but my friend recognized the need for both of us to stop for a minute and just rest.

Given time to reflect on that instant in my history, I cannot help but be grateful to my friend for the care he had for me. I would not have admitted the need to rest. As a "Type-A" person, my mind had already jumped ahead to the next dozen tasks we needed to accomplish. My friend however, recognized that if I didn't take a break, my energy and attitude would continue to be depleted.

A true friend will recognize when his or her beloved is in need of anything. Whether it is a word of encouragement, a hug, a rebuke or simply a moment of precious time, a friend is able to recognize a need. Friendships can obviously grow out of any number of things – struggles, loneliness, common likes (or dislikes), etc… – or simply out of circumstances. I find one of the most interesting relationships in Scripture to be the one between Ruth and Naomi.

For ten years, Ruth (whose name in Hebrew actually sounds like the word for friendship) had been the daughter in law of Naomi. After the death of her husband and two sons, Naomi decided to return to her native land of Bethlehem in Judah. She started out with her two daughters in law, Ruth and Orpah, but then decided they should return to Moab. Although Orpah decided to return home, Ruth replied with a deeply heartfelt response.

> *Don't urge me to leave you or to turn back from you. Where you go I will go, and where you stay I will stay. Your people will be my people and your God*

> *my God. Where you die I will die and there I will be buried. May the LORD deal with me, be it ever so severely, if anything but death separates you and me.* Ruth 1: 16-17

Ruth was now a part of Naomi's family. Death had technically given her cause for separation, but she chose to value friendship and relationship over the security offered in returning home. She knew that Naomi needed her and she cared for Naomi. She felt the calling of God upon her heart and acted on it. God recognized this act of love, as did the people in Bethlehem. When Boaz noticed an unusual face in the crowd of harvesters, he inquired of a servant who she was. When the servant told him she was the Moabitess, Boaz knew exactly who she was and what she had done.

> *Boaz replied, "I've been told all about what you have done for your mother-in-law since the death of your husband – how you left your father and mother and your homeland and came to live with a people you did not know before. May the LORD repay you for what you have done. May you be richly rewarded by the LORD, the God of Israel, under whose wings you have come to take refuge."* Ruth 2: 11-12

The rest of the story, as they say, is history. Ruth's faithfulness to the calling of God upon her heart and desire to help her friend and mother-in-law resulted in her becoming part of the family of Boaz's family and the family of God. Ruth is even listed in the lineage of Christ in the Gospel of Matthew.

The challenge of relationships in the family of God and, more specifically, in the church is one in which we must grow closer to God and to one another as brothers and sisters in Christ.

The relationship with God is fostered in prayer. It is our lifeline to God. We must be in consistent and continual conversation with God if we are going to be empowered and protected. Relationships deepen with time together.

Be joyful always; pray continually; give thanks in all circumstances, for this is God's will for you in Christ Jesus. 1 Thessalonians 5: 16-18

As brothers and sisters in Christ, we are of the same family, God's family. An ancestry in God is spiritual in nature and extraordinary in call. We are a called-out people, chosen to be co-implementers of His plan for our lives.

The only thing that counts is faith expressing itself through love. Galatians 5: 6b

By absorbing the love of God for us and, in faith, reflecting that love in all of our relationships and to those we encounter, we are living a life that is pleasing to God. Imagine the impact if all believing Christians studied the Scriptural imperatives of the faith regarding our relationships with one another and consistently embodied those teaching every day of our lives! God would indeed be glorified.

Safety and security is not a factor when God is asking us to open our eyes and hearts in our relationships with Him. We should likewise be able to open our hearts to our fellow brothers and sisters in the faith without fear of ramifications. As you move into this section, pray that God will allow you to see any walls you have built or friendships you have rejected because of personal issues. What would God have you to do in those situations?

Guiding Principle
The only separation the Bible knows is between believers on the one hand and unbelievers on the other. Any other kind of separation, division or disunity is of the devil. It is evil and from sin.
Bishop Desmond Tutu

The Challenge of Leadership

When it gets down to the root of effectiveness, whether it is in the church or some other group of people trying to accomplish something together, it is the quality of relationships that makes the difference. The perfect plans will be thwarted if people are not wiling to trust each other and work interdependently. Leaders must work hard to build relationships in their churches. This includes both the vertical relationships between individuals and God and the horizontal relationships between brothers and sisters in Christ.

The following key questions are important to consider as we review the component of relationships.

- Why are relationships so important to the effectiveness of the church?
- How do we grow closer to God?
- Why is prayer important to the functioning of the Body as a whole?
- How can prayer help us to be more effective leaders?
- How do we grow closer to one another as brothers and sisters in Christ?
- What are some healthy models for human interaction and effectiveness?
- How does God admonish us to protect our relationships?

Moving through these questions and completing the exercises will help you to better grasp God's desire for us to work with Him and with one another as brothers and sisters in Christ.

Why Are Relationships So Important To The Effectiveness Of The Church?

Good relationships are simply indispensable to the effective functioning of any organization. **Leaders will only be effective to the extent that they have the respect and trust of those they are attempting to lead.** Leadership has changed in the last several years. Dictatorial leadership is no longer accepted within the majority of organizations in North America. The prevalent mindset of "question authority" has permeated the culture at almost every level. In this environment, TRUE leadership can no longer be assigned or elected. Trust must be gained and kept. In the Christian setting, relationship building must be intentional and consistent. This is a key component of the effective church and a most crucial component as we consider God's call to unity. Scripture, especially the New Testament, is full of exhortations challenging us to love one another and to learn to live together.

And the second [Greatest Commandment] *is like it: Love your neighbor as yourself.* Matthew 22:39

Love must be sincere. Hate what is evil; cling to what is good. Be devoted to one another in brotherly love. Honor one another above yourselves. Never be lacking in zeal, but keep your spiritual fervor, serving the Lord. Be joyful in hope, patient in affliction, faithful in prayer. Share with God's people who are in need. Practice hospitality. Romans 12: 9-13

Carry each other's burdens, and in this way you will fulfill the law of Christ. Galatians 6: 2

God understood that nurturing a healthy relationship with Himself and sustaining unity among believers would be our greatest challenges as Christians.

How Do We Grow Closer To God?

PRAY! To stay intimately connected with God, leaders must be in touch with their Father through consistent, meaningful and intentional prayer. If leaders have any hope of effectively leading people, they must be in touch with God continuously. A man or woman that does not have a vital, life-dependent prayer life will not be effective as a leader in the church.

> *Men and women who know their God are men and women who pray, and the first point where their zeal and energy for Gods' glory come to expression is in their prayers...the invariable fruit of true knowledge of God is energy to pray for God's cause – energy, indeed, which can only find an outlet and a relief of inner tension when channeled into such prayer – and the more knowledge the more energy! By this we test ourselves...If...there is in us little energy for such prayer, and little consequent practice of it, this is a sure sign that as yet we scarcely know our God.*
> <u>Knowing God</u>, J. I. Packer

READ! To stay intimately connected with God, leaders must be in touch with their Father through consistent, meaningful and intentional study of Scripture. A key way to listen to God and to seek His instructions is to read His written word to us. A man or woman that does not have a frequent and passionate study time will not be effective as a leader in the church.

> *But as for you, continue in what you have learned and have become convinced of, because you know those from whom you learned it, and how from infancy you have known the holy Scriptures, which are able to make you wise for salvation through faith in Christ Jesus. All Scripture is God breathed and is useful for teaching, rebuking, correcting and training in righteousness, so that the man of God may be thoroughly equipped for every good work.* 2 Timothy 3: 14-17

WORSHIP! Once again, to stay intimately connected with God, leaders must be in touch with their Father through consistent, meaningful and intentional worship. Worship is to be both a communal event and a private habit. We worship corporately as we gather in prayer, praise, and proclamation of the Word and the celebration of the sacraments. We worship God alone in prayer, study and songs of praise. Our very lives are to be lived on a daily basis as if we are worshipping God. Work, in church or out, should be an act of worship and thanksgiving to God.

> *Let us draw near to God with a sincere heart in full assurance of faith...Let us hold unswervingly to the hope we profess for He who promised is faithful. And let us consider how we may spur one another on toward love and good deeds. Let us not give up meeting together, as some are in the habit of doing, but let us encourage one another – and all the more as you see the Day approaching.*
>
> Hebrews 10: 22-25

Why Is Prayer Important To The Functioning Of The Body As A Whole?

Without prayer, a church is like a body without a spirit; it is a dead, inanimate thing. A church with prayer in it has God in it. When prayer is set aside, God is outlawed. When prayer becomes an unfamiliar exercise, then God Himself is a stranger there.
The Necessity of Prayer, E. M. Bounds

That is actually a difficult quote to follow up with any sort of intelligent comment. E. M. Bounds has eloquently captured the essence of the necessity of prayer in the church.

Two kinds of prayer are important to the functioning of the Body as a whole: individual and corporate. If the individuals in the pews are not praying, they are not enjoying the benefits of a deep relationship with their Savior. If the church is not praying together, their fellowship is lacking an intimate way to stay connected to each other and to God. As Bounds continues:

> *As God's house is a house of prayer, prayer should enter into and underlie everything that is done there. Prayer belongs to every sort of work relating to the Church. As God's house is a house where the business of praying is carried on, so is it a place where the business of making praying people out of prayerless people is done. The house of God is a divine workshop, and there the work of prayer goes on.*
> <u>The Necessity of Prayer</u>, E. M. Bounds

Prayer needs to be continual in the church. Prayer needs to be continual in the life of the believer. It is key to a deep and growing relationship with God. Bounds effectively summarizes through these words:

> *Any church that calls itself the house of God but fails to magnify and teach the great lesson of prayer, should change the name of its building to something other than a church.*
> <u>The Necessity of Prayer</u>, E. M. Bounds

How Does Prayer Help Us To Be More Effective Leaders?

I am not a big fan of winter. While I love the beauty after a snowfall, the crispness of the air and face of my children as we breathlessly play in the snow, I loathe the scraping of ice off car windows, shoveling snow and the dirty mush created on the roadside by the salt and sand. It seems as if I need to constantly refill the windshield washer fluid because of the amount of fluid I need to use to clean the grime that builds up. Even after spraying, and wiping, it seems that there are always streaks remaining. This is a problem not even new blades can fix.

In the same way that vision is distorted by that filth, our spiritual eyes are often covered with the messes of the world. Living in a world of sin, we can lose sight of eternity ever waiting. Alarm bells ring. Sirens blare. Horns shatter the silence. The phone rings. Your shoelace breaks. Coffee spills on your shirt. A traffic jam made you late. The stock market dips yet again. There was another murder across town.

Sit still for a minute. Breathe deeply. Do it again. Tune out the noises. Is there a peace around you as you just sit? Can you not feel the yearning in your heart for something more? From the depths of your soul, aren't you passionately crying out for the embrace of your loving Father? This is why we pray.

If the local church had to eliminate all but one ministry that it performs, to be most effective, the one ministry remaining would have to be prayer. Leaders must be in prayer. Leaders must teach prayer. There is nothing more important that the church does. Prayer is not to be relegated to an occasional event or a random happenstance. Prayer must be intentional and consistent. God works. We pray.

How Do We Grow Closer To One Another As Brothers And Sisters In Christ?

Marriages are hard work. Any marriage that is strong is one in which both husband and wife work together for the betterment of the marriage and each other. It cannot be a one-sided labor. The joy of the marriage relationship however, overcomes the "down-side" of work. In love, any "work" is overshadowed by the togetherness of your God-given mate.

Families also are hard work. While working with your brothers and sisters in the faith, conflict is typically inevitable in some form or another. However, relationships are critical to the smooth operation of the Body of Christ. As we work together efficiently, there will be success in our work. The Bible consistently exhorts us to unity, to be of like mind and to agree on a common cause.

> *The central idea in Christian organizations is this – the unity of the body in Christ. All management techniques, programs, church growth formulas and other efforts to advance the work of the Kingdom fall flat if we are unable to find strength and encouragement from being united with other believers in Christ.*
> <u>Feeding and Leading,</u> Kenneth Gangel

What Is The Healthy Model For Human Interaction?

The church is a community. If the church is true to Biblical mandates, it is a community of believers whose priority is caring for each other and nurturing relationships. Effective churches understand this model.

> *Highly effective churches usually identify spiritual renewal as the ultimate goal of the relationships developed within the church network. Their perspective is that believers are to know, love and serve each other – just as we are to know, love and serve God Himself. To do so requires a purposeful and long-term commitment to relationships with other believers. The church, as the unifying organization, merely becomes the repository through which serious faith-based relationships emerge and are nurtured. Consequently, the local church can be defined not through its programs, buildings, events staff or teaching, but through the cumulative web of relationships that have been initiated and maintained among those who associate with that organization.*
> <u>Habits of Highly Effective Churches</u>, George Barna

Churches need to have members connected on three levels:
1. Celebration Groups – Celebration occurs as we worship together as a family in the faith. These groups are held together by a unity of

belief and purpose in the One whom they are celebrating. Although a worship service can occur with groups of almost any size, 70 or more is typical.
2. Community Groups – Teaching classes or ministry efforts occur when smaller sized groups (17-70) gather together to focus on a key issue or effort. Friendships are key to holding these groups together.
3. Care Groups – Small groups are necessary in churches as we seek to deepen the intimacy and interdependence of the individuals. We want these to happen regularly with groups in sizes of 7 to 17 people.

How Does God Admonish Us To Protect Our Relationships?

One of the greatest mysteries of the Christian life comes as we try to determine our role in the eternal scope of things. As Christians, what we do know is that God has a plan. And we know He has designated us to be a part of that plan. As His children, we are called to be His instruments. He promises us the power to get the job done.

Reality check – if that is the scope of our spiritual purpose as outlined in Scripture, how does it flesh out? How can sinful, selfish human beings ever attain a level of relationship with one another that will allow them to work interdependently with mutual trust, diligence and commonality of purpose?

Paul's epistle to the Ephesians is often referred to as the "procedure manual" for the church. The first three chapters clearly define our position in Christ Jesus. The next three chapters tell us how we are to function as the church. The bridge between the two sections is illustrative. Ephesians chapter three ends as follows:

> *Now to him who is able to do immeasurably more than all we ask or imagine, according to his power*

> *that is at work within us, to him be glory in the church and in Christ Jesus throughout all generations, for ever and ever! Amen.* Ephesians 3: 20-21

As the church, we have been promised the power to accomplish more for God that we can imagine. How does this happen? How can Christians appropriate this kind of power and be all that God is calling us to be? How can we insure that we are pleasing to God?

The key to our power and effectiveness as the "Body of Christ," is clearly defined in the next three chapters of Ephesians, and more specifically in chapter four.

> *As a prisoner for the Lord, then, I urge you to live a life worthy of the calling you have received. Be completely humble and gentle; be patient, bearing with one another in love. Make every effort to keep the unity of the Spirit through the bond of peace.* Ephesians 4: 1-3

Christians are called to a different way of living. Our strength and power come with the unity of our efforts as we work to accomplish God's plan as a community of believers. It is this unity that will assure our success. Ephesians 4, and many others of Paul's epistles tell us how we are to live. Each individual must take these inspired admonishments and instructions to heart. We have the power to change one person in our lives. That person is our self.

As we each determine to live each day "in a manner worthy of our calling," Christ's purposes will be accomplished through us and in turn through our churches. The alternative is also clearly defined in Scripture:

> *The entire law is summed up in a single command: "Love your neighbor as yourself." If you keep on biting and devouring each other, watch out or you will be destroyed by each other.* Galatians 5: 14-15

Action Steps:

1. In the same way you completed the examination in the preceding chapter, take the quick quiz on the next page. How can the scores improve?
    a. Average the score for yourself.
    b. Average the score among the other leaders.
    c. Average the score among the entire church.

2. Form and / or encourage an active prayer chain and regular meeting time within the church. Stress the importance of these ministries and call for members to attend as consistently as they would any other event in the church.

3. Develop a prayer card system to be used Sunday morning at worship and other meeting times. (Be sure to allow for private versus public requests.)

4. Emphasize from the pulpit and in every classroom the desire for unity in the body of Christ. Disunity is the tool of Satan and there is no greater threat to the powers of darkness than a church with healthy relationships.

5. Begin a Christian character teaching policy in all classes. We all need reminders regarding what it means to live a Christ-like life on a daily basis. Use Ephesians 4 and Galatians 5: 16-26 to give a clear rendering of Godly characteristics.

Personal Prayer Life:
___ 1. I believe that prayer should be an important part of my personal walk with Jesus Christ.
___ 2. I allocate some time each day devoted only to prayer and meditation.
___ 3. I believe that God hears and answers my prayers.
___ 4. I have concrete examples in my life where God has very specifically answered my prayers.
___ 5. I believe that my life is better and more peaceful when I am intentionally spending time each day in prayer.
___ 6. There are people in my life who do not know the Lord Jesus Christ for whom I pray on a daily basis.
___ 7. I pray for my pastor on a daily basis.
___ 8. I pray for the leaders of my church on a daily basis.
___ 9. I believe that my prayers will make a difference in the effectiveness and impact of our church.
___10. I believe that my prayer life is maturing at this stage of my life.

Prayer Ministries of My Church:
___ 1. Our church is praying church.
___ 2. We have a specific committee or team in our church devoted to prayer.
___ 3. We believe that prayer is the most important ministry of our church.
___ 4. When I am in need of intercessory prayer, I know exactly who to contact.
___ 5. We have a strong prayer chain through which I can report my prayer needs.
___ 6. We have a system set up that reports back to us the answers to prayers that we have offered up as a congregation.
___ 7. We occasionally have Sunday School Classes or special events that deal with the subject of prayer.
___ 8. Prayer is a critical part of my Small Group Meetings.
___ 9. I would like my church to help me gain a better understanding of prayer and its place in my life.
___10. I would like to commit to more involvement in our prayer ministries.

Talking Through the Boss

It's frustrating to work in the church. Sometimes it is just a big old pain in the rumpus. There – I've said it. Don't you feel better? I know I do!

OK – so if there is no Plan B, then why is Plan A so irritatingly hard? The answer is one simple three-letter word: SIN. Aside from wanting to let you know I have a remarkable grasp of the obvious, why do you think I bothered to say that? As we are talking about unity, we need to realize how vitally important relationships truly are to have and maintain with one another. We also need to learn how to talk with one another. God communicates to us through His word and the prompting of the Spirit. You never know – He may even some day just talk to you through a voice like He did with a man many years ago…

> *Before I formed you in the womb I knew you, before you were born I set you apart; I appointed you as a prophet to the nations. Now, I have put my words in your mouth. See, today I appoint you over nations and kingdoms to uproot and tear down, to destroy and overthrow, to build and to plant.* Jeremiah 1: 5, 9b-10

Before Jeremiah's cells began to form, before he breathed his first breath, before he took his first steps, God chose him to serve. Not only did God choose him, he appointed him as a prophet with incredibly powerful messages. God's own words would flow from Jeremiah's mouth as a means of warning people of the impending events.

God also commanded Jeremiah to do some pretty strange things as a prophet.

> *"Go buy a linen belt and put it around your waist, but do not let it touch water… Take the belt you bought and are wearing around your waist, and go now to Perath and hide it there in a crevice in the rocks"… Many days later, the LORD said to me, "Go now to Perath and get the belt I told you to hide there." So I*

went to Perath and dug up the belt and took it from the place where I had hidden it, but now it was ruined and completely useless. Jeremiah 13: 1b, 4, 6-7

"Go buy a clay jar from a potter. Take along some of the elders of the people and some of the priests...Then break the jar while those who go with you are watching..." Jeremiah 19:1b, 10

"Go to the Recabite family and invite them to come to one of the side rooms of the house of the LORD and give them wine to drink." Then I set bowls full of wine before the men of the Recabite family and said to them, "Drink some wine." But they replied, "We do not drink wine, because our forefather Jonadab son of Recab gave us this command: Neither you nor your descendants must ever drink wine." Jeremiah 35: 2, 5-6

The Lord used Jeremiah to communicate to His chosen people through some wonderful visual images. The methods of communication we choose are very important. We can communicate data (whether thoughts, messages or information) through various delivery systems (speech, signals, writing or behavior). As leaders, we must understand these various dynamics in order to be effective. Good leaders must be good communicators. Good communicators are sensitive to their audience regarding how messages should be sent and if (and how) messages are being received. Christ taught the crowds in parables constantly (Matthew 13:34) so that people would understand the message He was teaching.

The tongue is a mighty instrument of both edification and destruction. God calls us to use our tongues wisely in an edifying manner, doing no harm.

LORD, who may dwell in your sanctuary? Who may live on your holy hill? He whose walk is blameless and does what is righteous, who speaks the truth

*from his heart and has no slander on his tongue,
who does his neighbor no wrong and casts no slur
on his fellowman...* Psalm 15: 1-3

Restraint in our speech is a Godly virtue. Rarely does a person regret holding his or her tongue. We must learn to engage our minds before we engage our speech. Our tongues should be instruments of building up one another rather than tearing down. This building up edifies the Body of Christ.

Do not let any unwholesome talk come out of your mouths, but only what is helpful for building others up according to their needs, that it may benefit those who listen. Ephesians 4: 29

Our new condition in Christ gives us a remarkable power to rise above the sinful ways of our old self and allows us to conduct ourselves in a new manner. Christians are to act and react differently than the world. There are things that we are to do and there are things that we are not to do. Gossip, false witness, rumors, half-truths and innuendos have no place in the church. We have been renewed and we need to put on a Christ-like attitude in all that we say and do.

Work in the church is frustrating. The depth of our walk is reflected in our verbal self-control. Is the Lord speaking to you or through you?

Guiding Principle
Seek first to understand, then to be understood.
St. Francis of Assisi

The Challenge of Leadership

The potential for success in any organization can be determined by analyzing the systems that have been set up to insure healthy communication between its constituents AND the extent to which those systems are being used. Leaders must be aware of the tremendous impact that communication has on the church. Good communication systems and the diligent use of those systems can be the main factor contributing to church effectiveness. To the contrary, poor communication systems and implementation kill churches every day. Attention to communication by leaders in the church is critical.

A church that has struggled through the steps of developing a unified team with a common mission must strive to achieve and retain unity. Relationships are crucial and effective communication between the relationships is essential. In consideration of the elements of effective communication, we will address the following questions:

- How is the importance of communication emphasized in the Bible?
- What is the spiritual impact of communication on unity in the church?
- What are the channels of communication that need to be in force?
- What are the components of healthy communication?
- What are the dynamics of communication in the church?
- How is communication an issue of sensitivity for leaders?

"What we have here is a failure to communicate" from the movie *Cool Hand Luke* has become a common expression since the movie released in 1967. It has become a common occurrence in churches today. Addressing the elements of effective communication and using them to build unity will help strengthen and build your church.

How Is The Importance Of Communication Emphasized In The Bible?

Scripture is communication. The Bible itself is God's tool for communicating with Christians today. Jesus Christ is literally the embodiment of God's communication to us. John 1: 1 refers to Jesus Christ as the Word. He was both messenger <u>and</u> the message.

Scripture is overflowing with God's attempts to communicate to His children. He has even set the heavens to proclaim His glory and creation.

> *The heavens declare the glory of God; the skies proclaim the work of His hands. Day after day they pour forth speech; night after night they display knowledge. There is no speech or language where their voice is not heard. Their voice goes out into all the earth, their words to the ends of the world.* Psalm 19: 1-4b

Unfortunately, it is also overflowing with our failures to listen. God, through the prophet Jeremiah, proclaimed the failure on our parts to hear His commandments and obey His will. (See Matthew 13: 13 also.)

> *Hear this, you foolish and senseless people, who have eyes but do not see, who have ears but do not hear.* Jeremiah 5: 21

The spiritual impact of effective communication is expressed in God's story describing the Tower of Babel. It is clear through this story that God understands the powerful implications of people and their ability to clearly communicate.

> *Now the whole world had one language and a common speech. As men moved eastward, they found a plain in Shinar and settled there. They said to each other, "Come, let's make brick and bake them thoroughly. They used brick instead of stone, and tar for*

mortar. Then they said, "Come, let us build ourselves a city, with a tower that reaches to the heavens, so that we may make a name for ourselves and not be scattered over the face of the whole earth." But the LORD came down to see the city and the tower that the men were building. The LORD said, "If as one people speaking the same language they have begun to do this, then nothing they plan will be impossible for them. Come let us go down and confuse their language so they will not understand each other." So the LORD scattered them from there over all the earth, and they stopped building the city. Genesis 11: 1-8

The ramifications in this passage are tremendous. When we are truly communicating, there is nothing that we cannot do. In the account of the Tower, the communication and effectiveness of the people was leading to accomplishment that was contrary to God's plan. God quickly blocked their success by destroying their ability to communicate and scattered people all over the earth. This moving of God serve to further His Kingdom of God and His plan.

What Is The Spiritual Impact Of Communication On Unity In The Church?

As we grasp the relationship between good communication and effectiveness, we must focus on enhancing and protecting good lines of communication. A good example of the strategic use of communication can be represented in the history of military conflicts. In 1990 and again in 1998, allied military forces were called upon to suppress material threats in Iraq and Kosovo. Understanding the correlation between good communication and strategic effectiveness, the first thing that the American forces did was to destroy the enemy's ability to communicate. When we cannot communicate effectively, we cannot accomplish our work.

Communication is the second component on the architectural level of unity in the Ten Components of the Effective Church. Communication is the central dimension of unity because it is a key to healthy and vital functioning in all organizations. Communication is central in the entire pyramid of Effectiveness because without it, our architecture will fall.

When a church has embraced its mission, when it is motivated, obedient, understands its vision and has a Godly attitude, its potential for remarkable success is established. That potential will only be realized as the church stands unified. However, we must be ever vigilant. As Peter paints the picture:

> *Be self-controlled and alert. Your enemy the devil prowls around like a roaring lion looking for someone to devour.* 1 Peter 5: 8

Peter was well aware of the impact Satan could have on his own life.

> *Simon, Simon, Satan has asked to sift you as wheat. But I have prayed for you, Simon, that your faith may not fail. And when you have turned back, strengthen your brothers.* Luke 22: 31-32

Satan understands that the church can be paralyzed by broken and misdirected communication. His work is to destroy unity and foster distrust. He is a master at his art. He does not hesitate to do whatever he can whenever he can to block us from working with one another. The leadership of every church must be on guard against disunity, damage to relationships and communication failures. Leaders must be on their knees in prayer for themselves and for their fellow leaders. Standing united begins after we are united on our knees.

What Are The Channels Of Communication That Need To Be In Force?

The channel of communication that must be in place is

between an individual and God. The communication between an individual believer and the Creator is crucial to one's walk. Without talking to the One who gave life, we cannot hope to live the abundant life!

Healthy communication in the church at the functional level is dependent on two-way communication between at least three specific groups. In most church settings, the groups include the professional staff, the lay leadership of the church and the congregation. To keep each of the church's constituencies "in sync," intentional effort is required to make sure that channels of communication have been established for both sending and receiving information. Of course, there needs to be good communication within each of these groups as well.

The key is establishing channels of communication that everyone in the church understands. If there is a conflict between staff members, what route should one pursue? Should two members of the church enter into a dispute, how should that dispute be resolved (especially in accordance with Matthew 18: 15-17)? How are different ministries able to get their own messages out to the congregation at large?

In addition, the use of these channels of communication needs to be consistently encouraged and sanctioned. Communication is an on-going process – not a singular event. The life of the church is dependent on healthy channels of communication.

Evaluation of these channels of communication is also a necessary step to effectiveness. The church that is struggling within its ministries or in its relationships may need to take a step back and evaluate their communication channels. Sometimes, it may even take an objective third party to observe and recommend changes to truly become effective communicators.

What Are The Components Of Healthy Communication?

In its simplest form, communication can be represented by two cans and a string. It is all we need to get a message from one person to another. The two cans represent:

- A place where the message originates (sender)
- A vehicle for transferring the message between the sender and the recipient (delivery system)
- A place where the message is to be received (receiver)

Obviously, the components are quite simple. The dynamics however, are a much more critical phenomenon.

What Are The Dynamics Of Communication In The Church?

If the representation of communication is so simple, why do we so often have a breakdown in communication? The point where the message is sent and the point where the message is received too often conflict. There are several opportunities for this breakdown to occur.

1. Message never sent – This is obviously a total failure and oftentimes incredibly damaging to unity. Messages are not sent for several reasons, including:
   a. Innocent negligence – "We simply forgot to tell you."
   b. Habitual insensitivity – "I didn't realize you would be interested in this."
   c. Flagrant malicious intent – "They don't need to know."
2. Wrong message sent – "We had no idea that this meeting was to be as important as it turned out to be."
3. Wrong delivery system used – "I know the information was in the bulletin last week, but we were out of town last week."
4. Message recipient not listening – "There is so much irrelevant information in the bulletin each week, that we have trained ourselves not to read any of it."
5. Wrong message received – "We know that's what you said, but we know your motives and how you operate. That's not what you meant."

Obviously, with so many opportunities for breakdown, communication channels must be worked on very carefully. In marketing efforts, the standard is three vehicles. Tell them once, tell them again and then tell them one more time. Often, the vehicle itself will often vary as well. It is typical to reach out to the auditory learners through verbal messages (radio, television, word of mouth, etc...) as well as the visual learners through written messages (newspapers, magazines, billboards, etc...).

In the church, we need to remember the many potential messages and receiving styles that exist. Is this important enough to put in the already full bulletin? Does it necessitate a word from the pastor? Should it be communicated through Sunday School classes or small groups? Would a poster(s) be appropriate? Is your church "wired" for email messages to congregants? **Our goal needs to be effective communication.** Our vehicle therefore should be consistent to achieve our goal.

How Is Communication An Issue Of Sensitivity For Leaders?

Good communication is intentional. It is built on mutual trust. We need to constantly be considering the importance of our messages, the listening propensity of our audience and the appropriate methods of delivery. Messages sent that are not properly received are often worse than messages that are never sent at all.

Communication is as much an art as it is a science. It takes a wise leader to grasp the necessity of continuously improving the vehicles of communication. It takes an ever-vigilant leader to understand his or her people and their readiness and openness to be led. Good communication is the key.

> *If words are to enter men's hearts and bear fruit, they must be the right words, shaped cunningly to pass men's defenses and explode silently and effectually in their minds.* J. B. Phillips

Simply building systems and launching them will not be

enough. The systems and encouragement to use them must be sustained. Communication will deteriorate if left unattended. This is our nature.

Action Steps:

1. It is critical that a church understand its different constituencies and that it develop and maintain channels of communication between them. Channels must provide for two-way communication. Consider for yourself (and as a team) the various channels of communication and their effectiveness in both sending and receiving.
   a. Pastor & Staff to Lay Leadership
   b. Pastor & Staff to Congregation
   c. Lay Leadership to Congregation

2. Evaluate the understanding of your church at large regarding the channels of communication. Solicit input from the congregation regarding their opinion of communication in the church. What is effective and what is not? What new ideas do they have for communicating? In what ways can they take ownership of these ideas?

3. Create a structure for evaluating all communication in a given time period (two weeks or a month – depending on the church size). What succeeded? What communication / methods of communication could have been eliminated? Could any of it have been shortened (brevity often increases likelihood of being read)?

4. Go high-tech. Consider the future possibilities of technology for email broadcasting and web site use. As more homes and businesses become "wired," the ease of effectively and quickly communicating will be phenomenally increased. Once again, consider the gifts and talents of those in your church. For which person could this become a ministry?

Who's the Boss?

Order. Chaos. Arrangement. Mix-up. Sequential. Muddle. Which words make you think of God? Any student of Scripture will know that our God is a God of order. From the beginning of all things, God has had in place a plan and a structure for accomplishing His perfect will. His plan is perfect. Ours will probably not be.

I have often been described as a Type-A person. I like order. However, this unfortunately often results in control issues. It can be tough to release things in spite of the capableness and talent of so many people around me. Although I am getting better, I often don't even see the problems I am causing myself (and others) until I am overwhelmed with too much "busyness."

Once again, God, in His wisdom, has provided me with my own personal lesson from Scripture. (Does it apply to you also?)

> *Moses' father-in-law replied, "What you are doing is not good. You and these people who come to you will only wear yourselves out. The work is too heavy for you; you cannot handle it alone. Listen now to me and I will give you some advice, and may God be with you. You must be the people's representative before God and bring their disputes to Him. Teach them the decrees and laws, and show them the way to live and the duties they are to perform. But select capable men from all the people – men who fear God, trustworthy men who hate dishonest gain and appoint them as officials over thousands, hundreds, fifties and tens. Have them serve as judges for the people at all times, but have them bring every difficult case to you; the simple cases they can decide themselves. That will make your load lighter, because they will share it with you. If you do this and God so commands, you will be able to stand the strain, and all these people will go home satisfied.* Exodus 18: 17-23

Think you have it rough? Moses was the leader over thousands upon thousands of people who had just left their homes and were marching through the desert. Imagine the lines of people coming to him to complain about everything. "My lambs are getting mixed in with someone else's flock." "The children camped next to us are too rowdy." "The family in front of us left a dirty campsite." "There's too much sand." "Can't you do something about this sun?" The problems must have been overwhelming!

(There is an interesting thing to note about this story. Moses, the great leader who had defeated Pharaoh, could not solve this problem by himself! It took the wisdom of an outsider to point out what should have been obvious. Do you have a method in place for evaluation from an "outsider's perspective?")

One of the guiding principles of the faith is the principle of **the priesthood of believers**. The work that God has ordained for each church is much more than the active "20%" can handle and certainly too much for a pastor to accomplish alone. When wandering in the desert, Moses – the leader – felt the responsibility to do it all. Providentially, his father-in-law Jethro helped him to see the wisdom of delegation.

As we have mentioned before, the Ten Components of the Effective Church build upon one another. When we are building a building that we want to last, we must first focus on the foundation. Without stability and solid footing, those things that we build are doomed to fall. The strong foundation of God's vision for our churches must be effectively built. Building a strong structure of systems, procedures, organizational relationships, clearly defined roles and assimilation sets the stage for church health. A sound Godly structure will also hold up to the inevitable storms that face all churches throughout their histories.

> *Therefore everyone who hears these words of mine and puts them into practice is like a wise man who built his house on the rock. The rain came down, the streams rose, and the winds blew and beat against that house; yet it did not fall, because it had its foundation on the rock.* Matthew 7: 24-25

It is sometimes difficult to accept, but rules are actually a good thing. They protect us. They guide us. They let us know the boundaries. They help us to operate efficiently and effectively. God is a God of rules and discipline.

Psychologists did an experiment several years ago. They observed children playing in a beautiful square-shaped park area. Four very busy streets on each side surrounded the park. The children all stayed in the center of the park to play on the playground structure in the center of the park – in spite of the grass available for them to run in and trees on which to climb. After observing the children for a time, they had a fence erected on the boundary of the park area. Suddenly the children were running everywhere in the park, climbing trees and even the fence!

What made the remarkable difference possible? Boundaries. God, in His remarkable wisdom, provides us with our own set of rules so that we know exactly how far we can go and still be safe. As a church, we can operate with unlimited excitement and freedom provided we remain within His boundaries.

Do not be afraid of implementing a solid structure in the church. Many individuals fear that structure will limit the working of the Holy Spirit. Is it not incredibly egotistical to think that anything we do will prevent the Spirit from moving where He wants to move? In my experience, those who fear structure oftentimes actually fear a lack of losing control. In fact, the freedom structure provides actually opens the door for greater ministry opportunities. Hence, the Spirit will only be able to do greater things!

Structure provides us with a wonderful opportunity to serve our Creator and accomplish what He has ordained for us. Time spent developing a Godly structure for our church will both enhance and protect our unity as we work together. Rules are both a good thing <u>and</u> a God thing!

Guiding Principle
Be militant! Be an organization that is going to do things!
Woodrow Wilson

The Challenge of Leadership

Don't fall asleep! The challenge of leadership in building an effective structure is not only a good thing – it is a God thing! As we have just stated, the tendency of many leaders is to want to ignore this vital component. However, effective church leaders take the time to build an organizational structure that will support them in accomplishing the programs and ministries that God has ordained for them in an efficient and productive manner. As churches grow, the development of an efficient operating structure is essential.

- Why is it important to be organized as we accomplish the work of the church?
- What are the essential elements of effective leadership development?
- What are the advantages of an organizational chart?
- Why procedures and by-laws?
- What are core values and why is it important to establish them?
- How do we go about defining roles for all leadership positions?
- What is the relationship between spiritual gifts and church effectiveness?
- Why is it important to have a system for moving people through the discipleship process?

Structure will be more beneficial if it is established in anticipation of growth and the expansion of ministries rather than in response to them. It is the responsibility of visionary leaders to put the structures in place that will support the specific plan that God has created for the church.

Why Is It Important To Be Organized As We Accomplish The Work Of The Church?

<u>To accomplish God's work excellently, we should organize efficiently to get the most out of the human resources that God has provided.</u> God does not ask the church to do anything that He has not already given it the resources to accomplish. Therefore, if the church is having difficulty, perhaps it is because we simply have not been able to properly mobilize those who are called to serve.

As we study the church, one of the most remarkable phenomena is its organizational structure. Consider the work of your church. What are the duties that need to be accomplished each week, month or quarter? Consider the basics (from cleaning to bulletin preparation) to the complex (counseling to tax reporting issues). If those who are gifted are not serving in the proper roles, it is no wonder things are difficult!

Most churches have shifted many of the organizational responsibilities to the pastor who is often untrained and unskilled in those areas. Many pastors have reported feeling forced into the administrative arena. Churches are usually gifted with well-trained, experienced and effective leaders from highly organized and structured secular professions. The irony is that these spiritually chosen church leaders often do not transfer their leadership roles in the church. This is an enigma that many churches need to address. The more organized, efficient and structurally balanced the church is, the more time it will have to spend on life-changing ministry rather than dulling "ministrivia."

Personally, I am not a great number cruncher. I am good at analyzing some statistical data, following trends and forecasting ahead. However, I would be bored silly by balancing a checkbook. It would take me twice as long to do it than someone who has a penchant for numbers. Therefore, wouldn't my church be foolish to put me in charge of the checkbook? Wouldn't I be foolish to accept that role?

The responsibility flows two ways. If the church knows someone is not gifted, that person should not be forced into a role that would be in opposition of his or her gifts. In the same light, if an individual knows that they have no business filling a certain role, they should not attempt to force themselves into accepting such a position. A square peg will simply not fit into a round hole.

What Are The Essential Elements Of Effective Leadership Development?

Leadership is cultivating in people today, a willingness on their part to follow you into something new for the sake of something great.

Daniel Brown

The question to answer is this: What method will we use to intentionally train our leaders how to lead? The most crucial step to assure a healthy organization is to establish a good plan and system for leadership development. There are seven essential elements involved in the effective development of leadership in the church.

- **Identify** – Choose your leaders based on God's criteria, not just the leadership criteria of the world. Make sure you give plenty of time to the process and identify and "test" potential leaders long before they might be called.
- **Enlist** – Develop a comprehensive plan and schedule for choosing your leadership and make sure that the entire congregation understands it.
- **Equip** – Make sure your potential leaders know what will be expected of them and give them the training they need to do the job well. Jesus invested much of His time to training and equipping His leadership team, the disciples.
- **Empower** – Give leaders real responsibility and then trust that they will get the job done well. Nothing demoralizes leaders more than receiving a job to do and then having it done for them by the original delegator to make sure it was done "correctly."
- **Engage** – Be sure to use your leaders in a significant and effective way. The more important the job is perceived to be, the more commitment will be dedicated to it. The successful

completion of jobs will engender increased confidence, the willingness to take on more assignments and future success.
- **Encourage** – Make sure your leaders understand that you will be praying for them and encouraging them as they successfully accomplish their work. Good work should always be acknowledged.
- **Evaluate** – We all need feedback. Develop a system for honestly evaluating your leaders on an on-going basis. Accountability will stimulate action.

There is no correlation between potential and performance. There are lots of people with potential that do nothing with it. What counts is performance. GREAT LEADERS DO SOMETHING.

Peter Drucker

What Are The Advantages Of An Organizational Chart?

It's Christmas Eve and your task is to put together a child's bicycle. However, the directions are missing. You know what the end result is supposed to look like, but you can't figure out how the parts that are before you will magically pull themselves together to form that picture-perfect image.

Much like those missing bicycle directions, the church needs to have specific directions to determine how to put things together to fulfill God's plan. In order to determine the relational structure required to get the job done, every church – no matter what size – should develop an organizational chart. The importance of such a tool will only increase exponentially as the size of the church grows. The lack of such a chart will serve only to confuse and misdirect efforts along the path.

The organizational chart performs at least two functions:

- The chart makes it very clear who reports to whom and to whom each leader, both volunteer and paid, is accountable. One of the greatest shortfalls in the structure of the church

today is the lack of accountability. We don't do much simply because we are not being held accountable. Documented patterns of accountability will remedy this.
- A good organizational chart helps the congregation to know whom their present leaders are, who to go to with prayer requests, questions, problems or ideas. It will also let an individual know who to report to if the Lord is calling them to serve in a specific ministry. If we are not sure who is in charge, we typically go to the pastor, increasing his burden unnecessarily.

Why Procedures And By-laws?

There are few things more mundane and seemingly less "Kingdom-building" than writing standard procedures and by-laws for the church. This is a painstaking and tedious process. There are two important factors to remember during this process. First of all, once they are written, the task is done (except for possible futures adjustments and minor changes). Secondly, it will be extremely rewarding to have those established procedures and documents in place when difficult situations arise (and you know they will). Having negotiated "how we do things" before you actually have to do them will eliminate many potential future conflicts and "turf wars." What general would enter the war first and then attempt to draw up a battle plan?

When new leaders and staff people join the team, it is beneficial to hand them a document stating "how we do things" as they come on board. There will be no question down the road as to procedures because the "modus operendi" will have been established before they get involved in the system. Relationship building and communication will be greatly enhanced with a thorough understanding of your operational procedures.

What Are Core Values And Why Is It Important To Establish Them?

As you disciple current members and attract new ones, it is important that these individuals know where you stand. Another name for core values might be "position papers." Core values have also been described in the secular world as "things we are willing to die for." It should be stated that clearly in the church!

Ideally, core values are established in a church as part of their initial charter. With a bold declaration for absolute truth and Scriptural ideals, a church that boldly and bravely embraces TRUTH will attract people hungry for some clear guidelines and discipline in their lives. The unfortunate tendency is to back down or down play controversial issues for fear of turning individuals away.

The creation of a list of core values and their explanations can be an extremely difficult process for some churches. The effort to reach out without offending is a valiant effort. However, if we are so concerned with the opinions of the world, we risk being unfaithful to our Savior. In Matthew 23, Jesus presents what are commonly described as the Seven Woes. He describes the Pharisees and teachers of the law in detail as He cries out over their loss of heart over the legalism of the law. He uses terms to describe them like "brood of vipers," "blind guides," "hypocrites," "snakes," and "whitewashed tombs." If your church is unwilling to stand on a foundation of truth, it is better not standing at all.

How Do We Go About Defining Roles For All Leadership Positions?

During a recent anniversary celebration at my church, the keynote speaker was a member of the United States House of Representatives. Having attended seminary prior to being elected to the position, he remarked that he could not have gone into the pastoral ministry. He quipped, "It's too political. During an election, I only need to win 51% of the votes to remain in office. In the church, if only 20% of your constituents are mad at you, you're in big trouble!"

Every experienced pastor and lay leader knows the truth behind that statement. It is difficult to avoid upsetting someone in the church. As human beings, we obviously have our minor pet peeves and particular likes and dislikes. Whether we are making hamburgers or teaching God's commandments, the receivers of our communication will still process the information through their own channels.

As church leaders, we can attempt to avoid many of these seemingly inevitable problems as we define the expectations for each role in the church. Which of the following should come first?

A. Judging whether or not the task is being accomplished well?
B. Determining what the task is?

The answer to this question is obvious, yet rarely is the concept accurately applied. Whether we are talking about paid professionals or part-time volunteers, it is very important to define the job that is expected to be accomplished. We all have different expectations concerning what it takes to successfully accomplish every job. If roles are not clearly defined, we have set at the very least a course for frustration and at the worst complete job failure.

To assure job clarification, each worker must:
- *Know his task and believe it to be important*
- *Understand and support the objective of the overall program*
- *Be conscious of his relationship to other workers*
- *Be free from an atmosphere of intimidation*
- *Have a significant role in the group process*
- *Be alert to his responsibility toward maintaining a spirit of unity and community in the group.*

<u>Feeding and Leading</u>, Kenneth Gangel

Many people in the church operate at sub-par levels simply because they don't know what is expected of them. If we clearly define the task and the accompanying expectations for its success at the time that the task is assigned, most people will be very happy to work hard to get the job done. We want to know what our job is so that we can be sure when we are doing it well.

Therefore, as you are moving forward to define leadership roles, consider three basic factors. (This will be part of the action steps later.)

1. What are the roles that are needed in your church?
2. Based on the list of roles that are needed, clearly define the tasks that this position would set about to accomplish. (Include in this list the length of service required to accomplish the role. Is it a permanent position or short-term?)
3. Define the structure that will be used to oversee these positions. Begin at the top (pastor or church board) and work your way down. (Or begin at the bottom and work your way up! Who is in the position of serving each constituent group?)

What Is The Relationship Between Spiritual Gifts And Church Effectiveness?

The Christian leader understands that he functions in order to facilitate the ministry of others. He does what he must do in order that they may do what God has called them to do.
<u>Feeding and Leading</u>, Kenneth Gangel

One of the greatest responsibilities of the leaders in the church is to help the congregation to find their place of ministry. One of the greatest failures of leaders in the church is to fail to help individuals discover their spiritual gifts so that they may fulfill a specific role in the church.

> *It was He who gave some to be apostles, some to be prophets, some to be evangelists, and some to be pastors and teachers, to prepare God's people for works of service, so that the body of Christ may be*

built up until we all reach unity in the faith and in the knowledge of the Son of God and become mature, attaining to the whole measure of the fullness of Christ. Ephesians 4: 11-13

In order to facilitate this discovery and ministry placement, it is sometimes helpful to consider this relationship between giftedness and effectiveness in light of three categories:

- **DISCOVERY**: How will we help our members to discover their Spiritual and Ministry Gifts?
- **DEVELOPMENT**: How will we equip our members to fully make use of their Spiritual and Ministry Gifts?
- **DEPLOYMENT**: What system will we use to assure that our members are effectively implementing their gifts?

In terms of Discovery, there are several tools that leaders can use to explore and "test" members in the areas of Spiritual and Ministry Gifts. Because of the differences in denominations, one of the first places should be to solicit the help from your denominational headquarters. If that organization is unable to help, there are many books and supplemental resources available to do quick and simple tests to thorough examinations. The simplest method is obviously to just ask! Often the parallels between a person's likes and giftedness are remarkably similar (almost to the extent of pointing to a Divine Designer!).

Once these gifts have been discovered (or affirmed), the leaders must see that the gifts are developed. In which ways may a person with such gifts serve in the church? In which ways may that person serve the church outside of the physical walls? The shepherds in the church must tend to the care of their flock's needs and help them to grow spiritually and practically in service.

Would a doctor go through years of study and training and then retire to sit on the beach without ever seeing a patient? Of course not! The training and pursuit of the call is what drove them to the countless hours of reading books and interning at hospitals and clinics. In the same manner, a person who has been awakened into service should never sit back and wait for ministry to stumble over their pew. Leaders must make sure those gifted are deployed into service and receive continuing discipleship as they move forward. Don't start a fire and then ignore the flames!

Why Is It Important To Have A System For Moving People Through The Discipleship Process?

Without an intentional system in place, people will drift into the church and have a great tendency to drift right back out. An effort must be made to assimilate these individuals into the life of the church. To meld some teachings from Rick Warren and Bill Hull, we can look as someone is moved through the process to spiritual maturity.

The Lost (Lookers) come to belief through evangelism and the call of God upon their hearts (John 1: 35-51; Mark 3: 13). The New Believer becomes a Learner as the truths of Scripture are imprinted upon the heart (Mark 4: 33-34). This Rooted Disciple is transformed into a Laborer as they begin service to the King (Mark 3: 13-14). The Servant is then "employed" by the Master for work in the Kingdom (Mark 6: 7-13).

This is a process. With some excellent exceptions, many churches are either becoming "Lost-focused" or "Maintainers." In simple terms, the church either evangelizes or accepts the "movers" and "hoppers." In either case, if there is no guidance, once a person has become a member, that individual either seeks out a place of comfortable involvement or blends into the shadows. As time moves on, they either become entrenched in their place of involvement or drift out the door from their former place in the shadows.

As people believe they are being discipled through an intentional process of spiritual growth and ministry assimilation, they will feel firmly attached to the church. As they understand the plan and what is expected of them regarding their ongoing learning and ministry involvement, they will know that they are part of God's plan for the church. Church leaders – as shepherds – are responsible for the spiritual growth and nurture of their "sheep." An assimilation process will assure that you are accomplishing God's commission to make disciples. Help your people understand **from the**

beginning that your church is serious about disciple making. This attitude will please far more people than it will offend.

> *Church leaders may stir up opposition in the church in two ways. The first is by obeying God and leading the church according to God's agenda. This creates a great deal of friction. The other way is to be passive and allow the church to stagnate. This method causes the congregation to criticize the leaders for their lack of leadership. Either way, leadership faces opposition, so why not make your opposition count?*
> <u>The Disciple Making Church</u>, Bill Hull

Action Steps:

1. Does your church have a top-down or a bottom-up structure? Are the job descriptions of those in place dependent upon serving, leading or a combination of both?

   _____
   _____
   _____
   _____

2. Study John 13: 1-17. What effect does Jesus model of servant leadership play into your understanding of your role in the church?

   _____
   _____
   _____
   _____

3. Refer back to the section on defining Leadership Roles in the church. What sort of structure does your church currently have in place? Define the roles, positions and structure. Organize a chart to show the responsibilities of staff and volunteers.

   _____
   _____
   _____
   _____
   _____
   _____

4. Evaluate the awareness and training available for the discovery, development and deployment of Spiritual and Ministry Gifts in your church. Create a test (or obtain one) for evaluating the giftedness of the members of your church. How then can you develop and deploy the results of the test?

   _____
   _____

_____
_____

5. Hold a foot-washing service in the church. Allow the pastor to wash the feet of the leadership team and then have that team wash the feet of members. Although there is often A LOT of hesitation in the church, this event can have a powerful effect on church members.

Level 3 – Planning

Therefore, in the present case I advise you: Leave these men alone! Let them go! For if their purpose or activity is of human origin, it will fail. But if it is from God, you will not be able to stop these men; you will only find yourselves fighting against God.
Acts 5: 38-39

Only when the church is intentionally building and maintaining its foundation (Level One – Mission), and it is supporting and nurturing the second level (Level Two – Unity), can it consider the next level of the architecture (Level Three – Planning). The most important factor when considering building plans for your church is to understand that "successful" plans are God's plans.

We are all part of God's plan. We are instruments who need to operate according to that plan. If we do so, we will be successful. The key to discerning God's will for us and our churches is to stay in touch with Him – through the Word and prayer. He will show us how He wants His plan accomplished.

It is extremely difficult to accomplish things if we are not clear on what it is that we are to accomplish. We need goals. By establishing objectives to meet these goals, we place points on the horizon that allow us to focus. This will keep us moving consistently in a desirable direction. Objectives give us a reason for our actions. Effective churches establish clearly defined objectives.

If objectives answer the questions about what we are striving to do, strategies answer the questions as to how we are going to do it. Strategy puts flesh on the bones of our objectives. Strategies establish our marching orders. They are the engines that run the machine of effectiveness. Effective churches develop strategies to assure success in accomplishing their objectives.

An effective church understands the need to build mission and unity. The effective church will also understand that without plans, dreams of moving forward will have no tangible success.

Setting the Plan

It is a difficult challenge to assume the mantle of leadership. Unless you were the first person ever born (and there was only person that can claim that title!), someone was always there before you. According to those around you, the person who preceded you always seemed to do things a little differently. Occasionally, your method is better. More often than not, the former way was the "best way."

So what do you do when you are stepping into the place of someone who has lived the title of leader for the last forty years? How can you hope to "compete" with the legend that has come before?

Obviously you can't. Although we all want to make our mark and do great things for God, we must acknowledge that we cannot compete with the past. The tendency for human beings to look at the past with rose-colored glasses is a fairly natural phenomenon. A marathon runner does not concentrate on the pain of the last mile after crossing the finish line. The glory of the accomplishment is first and foremost in the mind.

Following in the footsteps of Moses, Joshua still had an incredibly daunting task ahead of him.

> *After the death of Moses the servant of the LORD, the LORD said to Joshua son of Nun, Moses' aide: Moses my servant is dead. Now then, you and all these people, get ready to cross the Jordan River into the land I am about to give them – to the Israelites.*
> Joshua 1: 1-2

This wasn't Joshua's first trip to the Promised Land. Remember – he and nine other men had been sent to spy out the land forty years ago. Eight of those men had been too afraid to enter and would not trust in God's protection and provision to help them. As a result, they convinced the people to turn their backs and we subsequently sentenced to wander the desert. Joshua and Caleb trusted God and now Joshua was chosen to lead the people into their new homeland.

Of course, the same people who had originally scared off the tribe of Israel were still there! Joshua and the rest of the people had not evaded the task of doing battle with them – it was just delayed. The task remained and now Joshua had to do it without Moses. Quite a task for your first assignment! What did God tell Joshua?

> *No one will be able to stand up against you all the days of your life. As I was with Moses, so I will be with you; I will never leave you nor forsake you. Be strong and courageous...* Joshua 1: 5-6a

With that reassurance, Joshua got to work. First he prepared the people. He provided them with a time-line of three days to pack up the camp (Joshua 1: 11) and get ready to cross the Jordan. Notice he did not get into great detail. He didn't know the plan yet! What he did know was that God was calling them to do something and he was going to see that it was done.

He then sent two spies to evaluate the land and get a feel for the mood of Jericho. Was this evaluation process really necessary? Over the past half century, LRM has had experience with churches of all sizes – from the small country church to the large suburban mega-church. One fact has remained clear. If the church takes the time to occasionally take the spiritual temperature of the members, it will only serve to strengthen the work down the road. Confirming that what we think to know is true is actually accurate can be incredibly affirming. (If the results come out otherwise, it is also wonderful to discover because you can be sure to do something about it!)

Joshua then started moving. The people broke camp and moved across the Jordan. This miraculous event was recognized and celebrated with landmark stones that would be a reminder for generations (Joshua 4: 21-24). The people also purified themselves to God's service. This was another remarkable event for its intense spiritual significance.

> *Then the LORD said to Joshua, "Today I have rolled away the reproach of Egypt from you."* Joshua 5: 9a

After celebrating the Passover, Joshua <u>finally</u> received the instructions from the Lord. As I'm sure you remember, the instructions were simple, but extremely bizarre. They were to march (quietly) around the city once a day for six days. On the seventh day, march seven times and this time blow trumpets and shout! If I'd received those instructions, I certainly would have questioned the messenger regarding his sanity! Joshua, however, was unquestioningly faithful.

Obviously, the story of Joshua continues on from there and Joshua continues to take the Promised Land for God's glory and the people of Israel. The objective was clear and simple – take the Promised Land. We will discuss strategy in the next chapter, but for now we will look at objectives and plans.

But the noble man makes noble plans, and by noble deeds he stands. Isaiah 32: 8

In Him, we were also chosen, having been predestined according to the plan of Him who works out everything in conformity with the purpose of His will. Ephesians 1: 11

Trust in the LORD with all your heart and lean not on your own understanding; in all your ways acknowledge Him and He will make your paths straight. Proverbs 3: 5-6

There is nothing that God does that does not fall within His eternal plan. From the beginning, man's creation was in conformity with that plan. His objectives were clearly preordained. Keeping spiritually focused and praying towards determining God's plan for our church as revealed by Scripture will then allow us to obtain God's full blessing for the church.

Guiding Principle
Objectives refer to the missional direction of the church stated in a sufficiently clear fashion that it is possible to know when they have been achieved.
Kennon Callahan

The Challenge of Leadership

If we expect great things to happen in and through our churches, we must plan for them to happen. Leaders must be sensitive to the spiritual needs of the congregation and the community, and intentionally plan to enhance the conditions of both. As overseers of the people of God, it is the responsibility of church leaders to set and accomplish objectives.

To that end, we will consider the following questions:

- Why is it important to intentionally develop plans for the work of the church to be done?
- What is the difference between a leader and a manager?
- What comes into play when determining objectives for our church?
- How do you determine the action areas that need to be addressed in the church?
- What are the criteria for good objectives?
- How do we set qualitative goal or objectives?
- What are the greatest challenges when setting objectives in the church?

Setting objectives can be incredibly mundane or it can be as exciting as anticipating the birth of a child. For the church that has embraced its God-given mission and is united in purpose, the thrill of setting accomplishable objectives is an answer to a dream. Time spent on the knees reaching upward to the King of kings and Lord of lords is now coming into fruition. Studying and struggling through seven components has now become joyous, as it is now able to future cast the reality to be. GET EXCITED!

Why Is It Important To Intentionally Develop Plans For The Work Of The Church To Be Done?

There is a story of a pastor who would enter the pulpit of his small country church every Sunday morning and wait for God to speak through him. He did no planning or preparation – simply opened the Bible and began to deliver the message. After years of this practice, he went home to be with the Lord. After entering the Gates, he expected praise for his willingness to be a vessel waiting to be filled with God's word. However, God asked him the simple question, "Why do you think I gave you six other days in the week?"

We can smile when we read that story, but the church that does not take the time to develop plans is operating as if only one day of the week matters. Effective churches determine how God wants to use them and set objectives to assure the accomplishment of God's will for them. No matter how sound the vision, without objectives developed to accomplish the vision, the church will drift. When you are not sure of where you are going, it is very difficult to tell whether you have gotten there or not.

If more churches intentionally determined their vision and established solid objectives to accomplish their vision, it would be astounding to see the impact it would have on the Kingdom of God. As leaders in the church, we must be setting the pace, charting the course and checking our progress. The church does not move quickly, but it must keep moving.

Ministry is not a matter of perfection but rather of progress. Effective leaders are out in front. That's the very nature of leadership. But if our lives grow stagnant and static, distracted by lesser things of this material world that stymie growth, then in time our sheep will pass us by.
<u>Shepherding the Church</u>, Joseph Stowell

What Is The Difference Between A Leader And A Manager?

Management is efficiency in climbing the ladder of success; Leadership determines whether the ladder is leaning against the right wall.
Stephen Covey

Management is doing things right. Leadership is doing the right things.
Peter Drucker

Efficient management without effective leadership is like straightening the deck chairs on the Titanic.
Anonymous

The world needs managers. The world needs leaders. The above quotes serve to illustrate the symbiosis between the two. In the church, it is a necessity to have leaders who are praying and earnestly seeking God's will for the church. In the church, it is necessary to have managers who are also praying and earnestly seeking God's will for the church.

In the work of the church, boldly moving forward to accomplish God's plan takes more than maintaining the status quo. Leaders must address the future and get on with it. Leaders are willing to set objectives and see that they are reached. Leaders are visionary.

In the work of the church, managers are needed also. "Manager" is not a bad word! Managers are typically more practically oriented and help to fulfill the tasks and complete the objectives as presented by the leaders.

Is one more important than the other? Excellent question – but the answer is no. A church, which recognizes the gifts of each person and allows that individual to serve using those gifts, will be blessed indeed. There will even be times that the manager acts like a leader and a leader acts like a manager. They are not exclusive traits!

What Comes Into Play When Determining Objectives For The Church?

It is often helpful to consider objectives as "action areas" in the church. These action areas are priority issues on which we need to focus our time and energies over and above the day to day functioning of the church. These action areas are special projects that help us accomplish the vision and assure the "big picture" effectiveness of the church. Before objectives or action areas can be determined, it is beneficial to go through a process to analyze where your church has been and where you are now. Assessing your past and evaluating your present will help you to make much more realistic decisions about your future.

For a great number of years, LRM has been offering tools (Church Impact Analysis, Spiritual Growth and Community Impact Survey, Interactive Master Planning) to churches to analyze the temperature of the church. Much like a visit to the doctor will help one to determine physical status and work through ailments, these tools serve the church seeking to honestly evaluate their spiritual status and work through difficulties. The results of these surveys have helped churches evaluate both where they are and where they will be going. A key factor of these surveys is their ability to record and analyze data anonymously. Unfortunately, in many churches, people are not completely honest because of the anticipated response. The depth of hidden emotion is sometimes rather shocking – but ultimately <u>very</u> beneficial.

A survey tool may sound time consuming (and it may be), but the efforts that will go into the study will greatly assist the church when determining objectives for future ministry. Remember, the goal is to make practical and realistic decisions for the future.

ACTION AREA INPUT CONSIDERATIONS:
- **Needs**: What are the needs of the culture and the community that the church is uniquely qualified to address? God placed the church where it is for a reason. Have you looked around you recently to assess what those reasons are? What are you able to do <u>today</u> to change tomorrow?
- **Accomplishments**: What are the things that have been done

as a Body throughout the church's history that have been very pleasing to God? What are the past and present successes?
- **Resources**: How is God uniquely blessing and preparing the church today with human, physical, emotional, financial and spiritual resources? These are the tools that God is providing to accomplish His plan for your church today. (I once worked with a church that owned a beautiful multi-purpose building. However, they did not want to risk opening that building to the public for occasional usage because they were afraid what would happen if people actually came!)
- **Perceptions**: What are the perceptions of the congregation concerning current ministry effectiveness? Perceptions embody self-esteem and are lived out everyday. Once again, please don't make assumptions about the perceptions. Consider an anonymous survey tool that will allow individuals to honestly contribute thoughts and opinions without fear of response.
- **Barriers**: What things stand in the way of the church's progress as it looks to the future? Consider physical barriers as well as potential spiritual barriers. Lack of space is not as important as a looming theological battle.
- **Dreams**: What are some of the unique opportunities that exist for ministry if the horizons were unlimited? It is important to be both realistic and crazy at this point. The church is where it is for a reason. All too often, churches limit themselves by not considering the potential of a future with the Almighty God at their side. What can stop you if God is calling you to do something?

How Do We Determine The Action Areas That Need To Be Addressed In The Church?

Can you imagine decorating your house in purple? I don't mean a few things with some purple color in them. I mean purple countertops, purple paint, purple switch plates, etc... When building a new home, a woman told the foreman she wanted a very specific shade of pure purple to be used in her home. The builder questioned her and even ordered in some samples for her to better see exactly what it would look like, but the woman was very insistent. After making her sign very specific contracts, they built it exactly as she requested. When they were completed with the project, the woman was almost giddy with happiness at the result. While the builders could barely stand to work in the environment, the woman was bubbling over with joy.

So what's the point? In the church, we must be very careful to assess the pulse of the congregation. (This is probably starting to sound redundant!) The perceptions of the congregation are important to evaluate as you plan and move forward. When we are clear on what is wanted and sure of our direction, success in the future is greater. With this on-going evaluation, you can be assured of the continuing progress and support of your members. The body does not function well if one part is attempting to move at odds with the rest.

In order to determine your action areas, the following questions need to be addressed:

- Based on our purpose statement and our vision, what are the key ministries that we should be accomplishing as a church?
- What are the ministries that we consider to be most important for our specific church?
- Which of those ministries are we doing very well?
- Which of those ministries need more of our attention and work?
- What are the unique resources that God is providing to us right now?
- What new things is He calling us to accomplish?

Based on your answers to these questions and an analysis of your current situation, objectives or action areas that require your immediate attention will rise to the surface. These objectives will become the focus for the balance of the planning process.

What Are The Criteria For Good Objectives?

The key to church effectiveness and a healthy, vital planning process is to intelligently set objectives. The objectives should be realistic, clearly defined, reachable, desirable and measurable.

- **Realistic** – Too many church consultants evaluate churches and provide them with summary reports outlining hundreds of areas that need to be addressed. The reality is that there is only so much that a church can accomplish in a given time period. The realistic church prioritizes its action areas and attacks them in an order that assures success.
- **Clearly defined** – It will be impossible for your church to accomplish its objectives unless those objectives are very clearly defined. There should be no question as to what it is that you are trying to accomplish – before you set out to accomplish it!
- **Reachable** – A church should have a good enough understanding of itself and its capabilities to know what it can do and what it cannot do.
- **Desirable** – The congregation will devote its support and enthusiasm to objectives that they desire to accomplish. It will be extremely difficult to get your people to work towards goals to which they are not committed.
- **Measurable** – You must be able to know when you have accomplished your objective. This means determining measurable results and realistic time lines. If your objective is so vague that you will not know with assurance that it has been accomplished, it is not a good objective.

How Do We Set Qualitative Goals Or Objectives?

Christian Schwarz has written an excellent book dealing with the planning process in churches. The book is entitled, <u>Natural Church Development: A Guide to Eight Essential Qualities of Healthy Churches</u>. His premise is that there are eight phases of church life that are crucial to healthy church functioning. Regarding the setting of qualitative goals, he states the following:

> *When we set goals, we need to do so in areas we can actually influence. This is the main reason why goals aimed at increased worship attendance figures are often counterproductive. In contrast, the quality of the eight key areas of church life can definitely be affected by our work. What else, indeed, should be the goal of church planning, if not the continual increase of its quality?*

Determining objectives is interesting to think of in light of this quote. Too often, we follow a business model of goal setting and look for pure "numbers." (We want to see more people in the church. Tithing should increase the church budget by 25%. And so on...) But the principles that Schwarz is referring to with his eight key generic areas are a helpful model to give us concrete examples of qualitative and quantitative objectives. Consider:

- *Leadership* – *"By the end of the year, our pastor will be released from 20% of his regular responsibilities in order to dedicate this time to the training of lay workers."*
- *Ministry* – *"At the end of nine months, 80% of those attending worship services will have discovered their spiritual gifts and 50% will be active in a ministry corresponding to their gifts."*
- *Spirituality* – *"By February 1st, we will have decided which of the three lay workers under consideration will assume coordination of the prayer ministry."*
- *Structures* – *"By the end of December this year, we will have determined a point person for each of the nine areas of ministry our church has established."*
- *Worship Service* – *"From the beginning of next year, we will have a worship service each quarter which is specifically designated to reach non-Christians."*
- *Small Groups* – *"Within the next six months, we will*

divide our home Bible study with the co-leader assuming the leadership of a new group."
- **Evangelism** – *"By the end of April the church leadership will have identified which 10% of the Christians God has blessed with the gift of evangelism and will have had a personal conversation with each regarding this gift."*
- **Relationships** – *"After having studied the <u>Learning to Love Process</u> for three months, each home Bible study participant will agree with the statement: 'I am enjoying being a part of this fellowship more than in the past.'"*

Taken from: <u>Natural Church Development</u>
Christian A. Schwarz
Church Smart Resources, Carol Stream, IL 1996,
page 111

What Is The Greatest Challenge When Setting Objectives In The Church?

Six little letters have caused more fear than the plague, diseases and war. **CHANGE!** However, if you want your church to be different than it is today, if you want it to be more effective in saving souls, growing disciples and touching lives, if you want it to move forward under God, you must be prepared to do battle with the fearsome six-lettered monster!

Change is simply one of the most frightening words in the Christian vocabulary. People don't want to do things differently. Everyone jokes about the families always sitting in the same places every week for worship – but it is usually true! Change is even unwanted often when people are completely dissatisfied with the current state of affairs. Churches will nearly unanimously agree that they want to challenge their people to more intense prayer lives, or that they want to attract new families to their church or that they want to dynamically increase their outreach. But, many of those same churches are unwilling to change anything in order to accomplish those objectives.

Change is a good thing when it is embraced as a catalyst to discover and implement new and dynamic methods to do the things that God wants you to do. Accomplishing new objectives to impact the church will require change. The challenge to leadership is to teach and educate those objectives to the congregation in a non-threatening way so that they will be embodied in the life rather than rejected.

The goal is NOT to change everything (although this can be a fear). The goal is to have effective and life-changing ministries. In the next chapter, we will discuss exactly how to develop strategies to accomplish these objectives.

Action Steps:

1. As a church leader (or preferably, as a leadership group), complete the following:

    a. List the current strengths of your church.

    _____
    _____
    _____
    _____

    b. List the current concerns of your church.

    _____
    _____
    _____
    _____

    c. What are five areas in your church where most of your efforts need to be focused in the next 18-24 months?

    _____
    _____
    _____
    _____
    _____
    _____

    d. What is the one main thing keeping your church from moving forward at a pace that would be pleasing to God?

    _____
    _____
    _____

This exercise will help you to focus on the remarkable blessings that God is currently showering down on your church. It will help you to isolate and prioritize concerns. It will help you to target the barriers that are keeping you from moving ahead.

2. Plan an evening or weekend retreat devoted to nothing but developing an intentional planning process for your church. This endeavor will be extremely difficult if you attempt to accomplish it during the regularly scheduled meeting times.

3. Schedule a time to objectively analyze and profile the perceptions of your congregation. You cannot move forward until you clearly understand where you are today.

4. Subscribe to a planning system with steps and stages of accountability.

5. Commit to specific objectives. Agree with your leadership team on 3 to 5 action areas to which you will devote much of your time and energy as you plan for the future. Assign individuals with leadership skills and a real passion for each area to oversee the planning and implementation process in that area.

Spiritual Growth and Community Impact Survey

LRM has developed a very simple and very effective tool for measuring spiritual growth. By asking your members and visitors to evaluate their spiritual condition through the use of an easy to understand yet comprehensive survey, your church's progress will be easy to measure from year to year. The tool measures leadership effectiveness in nurturing spiritual growth and progress.

The Spiritual Growth and Community Impact Survey is designed to be administered to your entire congregation annually. Through the use of 36 straightforward "yes" or "no" questions and 4 demographic questions, the spiritual condition of your congregation is accurately gauged. 31 of the questions are standard. Your leaders develop an additional 5 "yes" or "no" questions that apply specifically to your situation. You also have the opportunity to ask your members to address one essay-type question in detail. Your members will easily be able to complete this survey in 15 minutes or less.

A second survey is administered to your leadership team. This survey asks them to consider each of the spiritual growth areas in regards to their expectations regarding the congregation as a whole. As an example, Question Five of the SGCIS makes the statement; "On average I spend 15 minutes or more each day with God in prayer." The respondents are asked to answer yes or no. On the leader survey, the leaders are asked to enter a number representing the percentage of the congregation that they would realistically want to respond "yes" to this question.

The analysis of the data captured using these two tools allows the creation of a Data Evaluation Report that generates a huge volume of data relating to 1) the current spiritual state of the congregation, 2) the leaders expectations in each spiritual growth category and 3) clear guidance as to where ministry efforts need to be placed. Through the creation of focused objectives for enhancing spiritual growth in specific areas, effective ministry can be accomplished. In subsequent years, as the SGCIS is repeated, growth progress will be objectively measured and compared to previous years.

Getting The Job Done

It's a beautiful day outside. After weeks of anticipation, you are finally ready to embark on a sail around the world. The ship's captain has promised you an adventure to remember. You have brought all your supplies aboard the sailboat and are now ready to launch. Suddenly you discover that the captain just bought the boat yesterday. In fact, even his title of captain is questionable! He has never sailed before and can't even swim. When you catch a glimpse of the book in his pocket (<u>Complete Dummy's Guide to Sailing</u>), you decide the time to disembark has come.

Something was obviously missing in the planning process. Although the time was taken to prepare oneself mentally and physically, it is still incumbent upon the one taking a long journey to make sure that all the strategies are in place to get the job done. Of course, the task is not an effort of just one person – no matter how much we want to do everything. Sometimes, there is more to the picture than we can understand and accomplish by ourselves.

The letters of Paul to Timothy (and the letter to Titus) contain the qualifications that are generally considered the benchmarks for leadership. However, they are also helpful to look at when considering the development of strategies. Let's take a look at the man to whom the letters were written.

> *Don't let anyone look down on you because you are young, but set an example for the believers in speech, in life, in love, in faith, and in purity.*
> 1st Timothy 4: 12

> *Stop drinking only water, and use a little wine because of your stomach and your frequent illnesses.*
> 1st Timothy 5: 23

> *For God did not give us a spirit of timidity, but a spirit of power, of love and of self-discipline.*
> 2 Timothy 1:7

> *You then, my son, be strong in the grace that is in*

Christ Jesus. 2 Timothy 2: 1

Based on these passages, would you consider Timothy to be a strong forceful leader, not afraid to assert himself? I would not. However, I do see Timothy as being one of the strongest leaders in the early church. Why?

First of all, he was young and yet he set an example. It can be difficult for a Christian to set an example when dealing with others – especially in all areas of life that Paul challenged Timothy. To be called upon to do so while serving as a younger person in a position of leadership can be even more difficult. Nevertheless, Timothy was able to follow Paul's instructions.

Secondly, Timothy was a timid person, subject to stomach ailments (possibly because of this very "nervousness"). As a result of these illnesses, Paul actually tells Timothy TO DRINK some wine to settle his stomach. In how many churches today can you see someone actually telling the pastor to drink a little and settle down!

The remarkable power that Timothy received came from the grace of Christ. Christ also granted Timothy a remarkable mentor to give him guidance and teaching for developing strategies while working with the church in Ephesus. Timothy began his journey with Paul when he was only about 15 years old. Timothy was with Paul on several missionary journeys (see Acts 16), was imprisoned with Paul (see Philippians 1:1) and was credited as the co-author of several letters (2 Corinthians, Philippians, Colossians, 1 & 2 Thessalonians and Philemon). Paul was able to teach Timothy about planning, conduct and service.

Today, we obviously cannot physically travel with Paul, but we do have the benefit of traveling through the Word and reaching out to him and other contemporary mentors for instruction. The moments of intimidation and fear that we experience are temporary conditions as long as we remember Who is on our side!

David said to the Philistine, "You have come against me with sword and spear and javelin, but I come against you in the name of the LORD Almighty, the God of the armies of Israel, whom you

> *have defied. This day the LORD will hand you over to me, and I'll strike you down and cut off your head."* 1 Samuel 17: 45-46

All of our strategies should be based on our faith that they can and will be accomplished in the name of the LORD. For this to occur, our plans must square up perfectly with Scriptural guidelines and spiritual motives. We must be sure that our plans coincide with God's plans.

> *Commit to the Lord whatever you do, and your plans will succeed.* Proverbs 16: 3

We develop our plans to the best of our ability, seeking to align the work of our church to what we perceive to be God's plan for our church. Upon completing our strategies, we commit them to the Lord. Human plans committed to Godly motives will succeed.

> *Finally, be strong in the Lord and in his mighty power. Put on the full armor of God so that you can take your stand against the devil's schemes. For our struggle is not against flesh and blood, but against the rulers, against the authorities, against the powers of this dark world and against the spiritual forces of evil in the heavenly realms.* Ephesians 6: 10-12

By filling ourselves with God's word and preparing for the daily battle, we will be prepared for the war. The spiritual dimension of leadership cannot be overemphasized. We must understand our adversary and be prepared to fend off his onslaughts. Strong churches with Godly strategies and the fortitude to carry them out will come under spiritual attack. Paul challenged Timothy to stay the course (2 Timothy 4: 14-17). He is doing the same to us today.

Guiding Principle

The typical church in North America is like a sailboat without a rudder, drifting aimlessly in the ocean. As if that is not bad enough, the winds of change and the currents of postmodernism are relentlessly blowing and pulling the church even further off course. I believe that the rudder that the church is missing is a good strategic planning process. Without it, the typical sailor – today's pastor – will find it difficult to navigate in any situation."
Aubrey Malphurs

The Challenge of Leadership

Strategy defines how we will accomplish purpose, vision and objectives. Leaders in the church are the overseers of the nuts and bolts of the planning process. They must make sure that the strategies that are being developed fall within the bigger picture of God's purpose and vision.

Leaders should work to include the entire body of Christ in the planning and implementation process. Successful plans include as many church members as possible. As the church subscribes to the concept of a community in action, its work will have greater impact.

As we are putting definition to strategies in the church, we will consider the following questions:
- Why is planning so difficult to accomplish?
- What is the difference between establishing objectives and planning strategy?
- Who should develop the strategies of the church?
- What are the principles of the planning process?
- What is the conceptual framework for planning?
- What questions need to be asked in order to develop winning strategies?
- What are the most common reasons for failure in the goal setting process?

Why Is Planning So Difficult To Accomplish?

Most people, when asked, will strongly agree that planning is an important exercise for every individual and organization. As individuals, we plan out our days – from what time we will get up to what time we will go to bed. We schedule lunch meetings, appointments and time to dedicate to specific tasks. In today's culture, we are even scheduling time to spend with family! As organizations, we often talk abstractly at great length about future dreams and visions. Time and time again, we hear churches paint great visions to capture the enthusiasm, yet rarely do those visions translate into concrete reality.

Through Scripture we have great reassurance of the future as Christ details in the Sermon on the Mount the glorious provision of our Heavenly Father. We are exhorted to not worry about our food, drink or clothing. Worrying cannot add anything to our lives. Today has enough trouble without worrying about tomorrow. Therefore, how can we say audaciously that churches should plan?

Remember the discussion about Plan B? There is no Plan B! We shouldn't worry about tomorrow, but we should plan for tomorrow! We are created to do good works (Ephesians 2: 10). We are created to go into the world and tell the Good News (Mark 16: 15). We are created to be witness to the world (Acts 1: 8). Although we can actually accomplish these things without planning, our activities can be much more fruitful if we do in fact prepare.

Planning can be so difficult for many because it is indeed projecting into the future. Most people like to deal with the here and now and then talk in general terms about the future. Action in the present can produce tangible results. Future casting cannot produce results until that future becomes a reality. If that reality does not emerge, we consider ourselves failures.

Another complication to planning is the "everydayness" of life. While we are so busy "doing," we don't look ahead. Problems emerge and we must take care of those problems before we move ahead. It becomes a vicious circle of problem solving and action instead of planning. If we had taken the time to plan in the first place, perhaps many of those problems wouldn't have happened in the first place!

Regardless of our reasons, planning is a prerequisite for effective church functioning. The church will do damage to itself and to those who worship in the building if the leaders fail to plan. We must overcome the difficulties and get to work!

What Is The Difference Between Setting Objectives And Planning Strategy?

Objectives answer the question, "What do we think God is calling this church to do?" Strategies answer the question, "How are we going to do it?" The most inspired purpose and vision and the most prayerfully derived objectives are of little value without the intentional determination to get the job done. The intentional plan to get the job done is your strategy.

When we enter the offices of churches across the country, it almost seems as if we are hearing the voices of thousands of tiny little voice screaming, "Let us out!" These voices are the voices of plans involving purpose, vision and objectives that have been living deep within the recess of church secretaries and pastors across the globe. It might be possible to publish a year's worth of newspapers if we were able to recycle all of that paper!

Seriously, the number of ideas and plans that have simply died from lack of strategies to get the job done is overwhelming. However, developing strategy takes the church from the abstract to the concrete. If we are clever enough to use the mental faculties that God has given to us, we will be able to develop the right plans to do the right job.

Who Should Develop The Strategies Of The Church?

Pastoring in the twentieth century requires two things: one, to be a pastor, and two, to run a church. They aren't the same thing.

Eugene H. Peterson

__Renewing Your Church Through Vision & Planning__

Developing strategies to accomplish objectives or action areas should be assigned to ministry teams or task forces chosen for the specific purpose of making plans and implementing them. **<u>The same body that will have to implement the strategy should develop the strategy.</u>** If those people do not have a stake in the plans and ownership in setting the check points and accountability, then there will be no responsibility for actually working to make the strategies come to fruition.

Honestly, this is one of the most difficult things for a pastor and leadership team to turn over to the lay people. However, if the master planning process turns into another list of "things to do" for the pastor and professional staff, the process will be more of a detriment to the church than a benefit. Consider the following statements from the book, <u>The Second Coming of the Church</u>, by George Barna.

- *Less than one out of every ten senior pastors can articulate what he believes is God's vision for the church he is leading.*
- *Only 5 percent of senior pastors say they have the gift of leadership. Most pastors thought they were neither called to nor divinely equipped for that post.*
- *A time-management study we* [Barna] *conducted among pastors showed that the typical pastor works long hours (more than sixty hours per week), but devotes less than ten hours per week to leadership activities.*

Are these statements contradictory to the earlier assertions that it is the pastor who must finally champion the vision of the church? No. The senior pastor must be the torchbearer leading the congregation ahead. The pulpit is the primary avenue of communication in many churches for communication of the Word and guidance in daily life.

The professional staff and lay leadership must also have a role in the planning process. It is their responsibility to help shepherd the flock. Much of the additional teaching and guidance will reach members through their efforts.

Congregational members are to do the work of the church. Leaders, in developing plans, must be bold, aggressive and willing to take risks. God has given your church exactly the leaders and team members that you need to accomplish His purposes. Successful churches are willing to eliminate pride issues and allow the properly gifted leaders and individuals to get the job done.

Again, the pastor must have a passion for the vision of the church if it is to succeed, but he does not necessarily have to single-handedly discern the vision and he should not be responsible for developing and implementing each and every plan.

A constant excuse for failed plans is to blame the failure on strategies developed by others. As they are given ownership in developing strategy, individuals will take responsibility for making those strategies work.

The difference between having a successful plan and another dead tree in a filing cabinet is ownership. Having the teams who are responsible in a ministry area develop the strategies and timelines for carrying out that plan will provide ownership. The support and guidance of the pastor, professional staff and lay leadership will enhance the planning process.

What Are The Principles Of The Planning Process?

After considering the "who," it is important to also look at the "what" aspect of the planning process for developing strategies. The "what" aspect will look at various principles that are important for the church leaders and lay participants to keep in mind as they move forward. Kenneth Gangel has detailed eight important principles that can be considered as map points for developing strategies.

- *Planning is an investment, not an expenditure of time.*
- *Planning requires careful attention to immediate choices because immediate choices*

> *greatly expand or narrow future options.*
> - *Planning is cyclically based on evaluation.*
> - *Planning demands acting objectively toward goal realization.*
> - *Planning helps us note the relationship between determining what we want to do and realizing that end.*
> - *In planning, specificity increases as the event draws near.*
> - *Planning requires maximum participation.*
> - *Planning demands that effort applied be commensurate with the results required.*
>
> <u>Feeding and Leading</u>, Kenneth Gangel

What Is The Conceptual Framework For Planning?

In high school, many of us were challenged to run the mile. Although my ability in traveling a mile is now relegated to walking instead of running, it is nevertheless is an interesting exercise to observe among young students. Of course there are those who consider the entire concept a futile expense of energy. For whatever reason, they choose to walk the distance. The sprinters, however, are off to the races from the start. Just like a cannonball, they explode out of the barrel with a fury. As the run progresses, they begin to slow down and feel the results of the distance. The wise runners set a pace for themselves from the beginning. Realizing it is a journey, they find a pace that will allow them to complete the task in a reasonable time without overtaxing themselves. As they pass the sprinters (now the walkers!), the probability of success will encourage them to continue.

What does this have to do with planning? It is a process, not a race. The journey will never be completed if the tasks are rushed or if an unreasonably slow attitude is modeled. Time is actually a very helpful tool in the conceptual framework of time. As timelines are set, plans take on an element of reality. Timelines establish targets that in turn demand accountability. If we say that we are going to accomplish something by a certain date, then on that date, we will have to take an inventory to see if we got the job done.

In a volunteer environment, this can be a frightening concept. When effort is expended without compensation, it can be very threatening to have someone checking on the progress. In order to be successful, timelines must be in place. Leaders in the church can help overcome the hurdle of fear by modeling their own efforts. By publishing objectives, strategies AND the timelines, others will see the work being attempted and the results. Honesty is crucial as is the celebration of success. Although this should never be done for pride or glory, if completed tasks are lauded in private and public, enthusiasm can be generated for moving ahead.

What Questions Need To Be Asked In Order To Develop Winning Strategies?

Sometimes it is difficult to think in terms of "winning" in regards to church work. Winning sounds "secular" and "worldly." Can a real Christian think in those terms? Can the church think in those terms? We <u>are</u> in a battle. We <u>are</u> in a war. We <u>are</u> in a race. As Paul stated so eloquently in his letter to Timothy:

> *I have fought the good fight, I have finished the race, I have kept the faith.* 2 Timothy 4:7

The words that we use are less important than the fact that we keep the faith. In keeping the faith, we recognize that there are times we are doing battle and it may be difficult. Our goal is to win – to win lost souls to a relationship with Christ. We have been commissioned to serve the King in spreading the news and we had therefore better be sure that we are doing our very best to serve the King with all that we have. If you are uncomfortable in thinking in terms like "winning" or "losing," you simply have two choices:

1. Redefine those terms to something with which you are more comfortable; or

2. Get over it.

The goal of the strategy setting process should be to develop a plan that you know you can accomplish with God's help. You want to develop a plan that you can accomplish within an acceptable time frame. You must want to achieve your goals and WIN!

Success will breed success. To be successful, it is necessary to be practical. Fred Smith, in his essay, *Secrets to Making Great Decisions*, gives the following list of questions to be asked during the decision making process. Keep these in mind as you develop strategies to win.

- *What are our options?*
- *Is this mutually beneficial?*
- *What is the risk?*
- *Is it timely?*
- *Do we have staying power?*
- *What are the long-term ramifications?*
- *Have we built in escape hatches?*
- *Have we asked for advice – after doing our homework?*
- *Have we validated our decisions in prayer?*

What Are The Most Common Reasons For Failure In The Strategy Setting Process?

Leaders generally attribute their inability to get things done to one of three areas.

1. **The lack of commitment to take the time to make intentional plans.** If leaders (paid and volunteer) are unwilling to pause from the everydayness of life to make some serious strategic plans for the future, it is no wonder that things will not achieve success. We can be intentional or accidental in ministry (and life). Which would God have you choose?
2. **The unwillingness to organize based on predetermined**

priorities. It is incredibly frustrating to actually form a plan and then have subsequent sabotage (intentional or not) to that plan. There are some individuals who are unwilling to speak up in a group if they disagree. They will then later seek to change or implement the opinions that were not expressed. This will result in difficulties and failure.

3. **The lack of discipline to act on the plans developed.** To have the privilege of working in the church is truly an incredible gift (even if it doesn't feel like it all the time). A volunteer labor force is also an incredible gift. However, if paid staff or volunteers are unwilling to move forward because of other priorities, action is necessitated by the leadership. Staff must be corrected. Volunteers must be encouraged and taught the value of their labor of service to the King. Discipline in labor is honoring Him.

Action Steps:

1. Evaluate your emotional condition and analyze your passion as a leader in the church. Make sure that you are involved with ministry that truly corresponds to your passion. If not, changes need to be made. God-determined ministry should be joyful.

2. Consider the following areas. Rank from 1 (highest) to 7 (lowest) where you spend your time. Estimate the number of hours spent in an average week (excluding sleep).

ACTIVITY	RANK	% TIME SPENT
Occupation	_____	_____
Family	_____	_____
Leisure Activities	_____	_____
Church Work	_____	_____
Personal Time	_____	_____
Community Activities	_____	_____
Other	_____	_____

   Spend a few moments in prayer reflecting on this list. Are there areas in which God would be better served if you shifted priorities or some time? Consider some personal strategies to change or strengthen those activities in the next twelve months.

3. Inventory Spiritual Gifts. As a leader, are you using your gifts properly? Do you have someone in your church that is helping individual members to find and use their gifts to the service of the King? Who is / should that person be?

4. Celebrate success! Publish the objectives, strategies and time-lines. After successfully completing an objective or meeting timelines on strategies, publish that information. Nothing is more refreshing, encouraging and satisfying than actually doing the things that you have set out to do as a body. Confidence will also be built and future successes assured as

you accomplish more and more of your objectives.

5. PRAY! Reinforce prayer and seeking glory to the King as you continue to develop and implement strategies.

Level 4 – Hard Work

Show me your faith without deeds, and I will show you my faith by what I do.

James 3: 18b

No one said this was going to be easy. To get things done, work is required. Faith and deeds go hand in hand. All the great planning in the world is wasted without the hard work need to bring the plans to fruition.

Effective Kingdom work is hard work. We must be diligent in constantly seeking God's will and working hard to accomplish it. An old parable says that God does indeed take care of even the smallest sparrow. But He does not throw the seed up into the nest. The work may be hard, but the rewards are beyond comprehension. There is nothing more satisfying. When we are positioned squarely in God's will, we are blessed because we are accomplishing the purpose for which we have been called.

You have been exposed to nine of the components to build an effective church. Motivation, obedience, vision and attitude are the foundation of an effective mission. With strong relationships, communication and structure, the next tier of unity has been set in place. Objectives and strategy have put flesh onto the planning process. Now it is time to get moving!

There is not a single plan that will be successful if it is never implemented. Effective churches will get the job done. Leadership Effectiveness Training seeks to help leadership to build an environment to create and sustain the action required to do the work.

Never fear healthy change. And do not doubt that generating a new dynamic effectiveness in the life of your church will require change. This change – major or minor – must be intentional.

Let's go to work!

Gotta Go To Work!

Imagine stepping up to the plate in the seventh game of the World Series at the bottom of the ninth inning. There are two outs and no one is on base. The score is tied. Everything rests on your shoulders because in the last inning your last pitcher was hit by a ball and broke his thumb. If you can't get on base, the game is essentially over.

As you dig in, you suddenly realize you don't have a bat in your hands! You turn to call time out, but the pitcher – realizing your colossal blunder – has already started the pitch. However, in his haste the pitch actually hits you on the arm. You shake it off and head to first. After you take a small two-step lead, the pitcher inexplicably throws over to first. His anger at his previous mistake is increased as the ball evades the first baseman. You sprint to second.

The first baseman heaves the ball well over the head of the second baseman and you proceed to third. The outfielder that has come in to back up the second baseman trips over the ball and it rolls into the corner. You have unbelievably managed to score the winning run without ever touching a bat!

Is it possible? Yes it is. Is it probable? Certainly not. Years of training and study would prevent experienced professionals from making such an obvious mistake. The three compounded errors by other professionals make such a scenario ludicrous.

And yet, at moments of weakness, is it not possible that even the greatest among us will make a mistake? We want to do great things. We feel challenged to do great things. We believe we are empowered to do great things. And yet...

> *Simon Peter asked him, "Lord where are you going?" Jesus replied, "Where I am going, you cannot follow now, but you will follow later." Peter asked, "Lord, why can't I follow you now? I will lay down my life for you." Then Jesus answered, "Will you really lay down you life for me? I tell you the truth, before the rooster crows, you will disown me three times."* John 13: 36-38

"You are not one of his disciples, are you?" the girl at the door asked Peter. He replied, "I am not." John 18:17

As Simon Peter stood warming himself, he was asked, "You are not one of His disciples, are you?" He denied it, saying, "I am not." One of the high priest's servants, a relative of the man whose ear Peter had cut off, challenged him, "Didn't I see you with Him in the olive grove?" Again Peter denied it, and at that moment a rooster began to crow. John 18: 25-27

Wondering where we are going? Peter was the most confident, brash and aggressive of the disciples. Typically the first to speak and act, Peter was vulnerable to the results of his hasty actions. (Stepping out of boats fully clothed was one of his most interesting tendencies!) This behavior and impulsiveness eventually resulted in a temporary separation from the other disciples (Mark 16: 7) and a beautiful scene of restoration with the resurrected Christ (John 21: 15-17). Regardless of the situation, this unofficial leader of the disciples was always ready to go when work was involved.

Does God expect us to really work?

The LORD God took the man and put him in the Garden of Eden to work it and take care of it. Genesis 2: 2-3

After this the Lord appointed seventy-two others and sent them ahead of him to every town and place where he was about to go. He told them, "The harvest is plentiful, but the workers are few. Ask the Lord of the harvest, therefore, to send out workers into his harvest field. Go!" Luke 10: 1-2

For it is by grace you have been saved, through faith – and this not from yourselves, it is the gift of God – not

by works, so that no one can boast. For we are God's workmanship, created in Christ Jesus to do good works, which God prepared in advance for us to do.
Ephesians 2: 8-10

    Peter exemplifies the type of attitude Christians need to have towards work. Granted we must be a little more patient, but we should be aggressively seeking opportunities to put faith into action. As we look at Peter's life and letters, we see his maturation from leap first – look second to a seasoned, dedicated disciple. The value of planning and moving with God became his method of operation. We pray. We plan. We act.

    Scripture is clear that God created us with a purpose in mind. We must be ever-seeking His will and His strength to accomplish that purpose. This is our calling as Christians. This is the work of the church.

Guiding Principle
Success is bearing as much fruit as possible given your gifts, opportunities and potential.
Rick Warren
<u>The Purpose Driven Church</u>

The Challenge of Leadership

Implementation is the final component in the architecture of the effective church. It can also be the most elusive component. No matter what goes on before and how productive our planning, it is all for nothing if we fail to implement those plans. Leaders must be the drivers that make it happen.

Leadership Effectiveness Training is a process. Through the ten components, the people of God learn how to be the church of God. The environment created by embracing this philosophy will build a church at is mature and impactful. Church leaders need to constantly be aware of the environment in their church and do everything they can to enhance it.

There are still a few difficult questions that need to be addressed in light of the work that is required to lead an effective church.

- Once a plan is in place, why is it crucial that we persevere?
- Why do we need to set up systems for evaluation?
- What about accountability? Is it a Scriptural phenomenon?
- When do we make adjustments to the plan?
- How do we keep the process of master planning alive?
- What will be our greatest barrier to success?

A house without electricity is livable, but not preferred. The job will not be complete until it has all the parts hooked up and running. As we complete our study of the Ten Components, remember the necessity of completing all the elements in order to have a properly functioning fellowship. With a driven and unified team, the atmosphere will truly be electric!

Once The Plan Is In Place, Why Is It Crucial That We Persevere?

Nine of the ten blocks are in place. The church is doing its best to create a vital and healthy environment as depicted by the pyramidal architecture of Leadership Effectiveness Training. To this point, the church will have committed an impressive amount of time, effort and prayer to seek God's will. You will have done your best to establish the foundation to yourself so that you are ready, willing and able to carry out His plan.

MISSION:

You will have determined and committed to your mission based on the **motivation** of the Holy Spirit, the **obedience** of your leadership, the **vision** given by God to your pastor and an **attitude** of excitement and expectancy.

UNITY:

You will have acknowledged the importance of unity and will have committed to build the necessary unity through a new emphasis on **relationship building**, the implementation of a good **communication** system and the development of an efficient organizational **structure**.

PLANNING:

By God's grace and direction, you will have isolated action areas or **objectives** that will move you forward. You will have built **strategies** to put feet to your plan.

HARD WORK:

Now you have reached the pivotal juncture of **implementation**. Can you and will you actually get the job done?

The voices of thousands of beautifully written master plans are still screaming out from the abandoned drawers of church filing cabinets across the country. This fact is the travesty of master planning. Finding a solution to this problem is critical.

PLAN YOUR WORK THEN WORK YOUR PLAN!

Master planning carried through implementation, will have a tremendous positive impact on your church. Master planning that stops before it is carried out can and will actually do more damage to your church and your people than if it was never embarked upon in the first place. Commitment to perseverance is crucial.

It's really a Catch-22. If a church fails to develop a plan, members and visitors alike will drift away due to apathy. If a church does develop a plan and yet fails to carry it out, members will drift away due to anger, confusion and lack of trust in the leadership. Given the choices, is it not best to develop a plan and then work the plan?

Why Do We Need To Set Up Systems For Evaluation?

A benchmark is the standard by which an individual may judge performance in comparison with other like circumstances. Businesses frequently use benchmarks from previous year's or sales representatives performance. It is a way to make sure that progress is being made and growth is occurring.

The church is an unusual organism. The "priesthood of believers" or the "saints called by God to accomplish His ministry" do much of the work. Serving in the church is a very lofty calling. However, if we consider the bulk of our workforce (using secular terms), that workforce translates into volunteers.

Most people want to do their assigned tasks well. They want to serve the Lord. However, given the opportunity to postpone or avoid the accomplishment of their ministry tasks, they will. This is the unfortunate result of the sinful nature.

Leaders MUST set up systems to check that goals are being accomplished. In the early stages of the plan implementation, the establishment of precedence is very important. Most workers will take their lead as to whether the process is serious or not based on early reactions to work completed or not completed.

Leaders must lovingly exhort those who are falling behind

and enthusiastically applaud those who are working according to the plan. All must understand that the work that is being done is important, significant and essential to the accomplishment of the master plan.

What About Accountability? Is It A Scriptural Phenomenon?

God gave His Word so that His people may know of His love and His will. It is the story of His historical dealings with His people. The main premise of the Bible is to reveal to us our need for God and His unconditional willingness to meet that need. We are a sinful people, incapable of accomplishing our own salvation. The Bible itself is a tool of accountability, exhorting us to press on.

> *Therefore, since we are surrounded by such a great cloud of witnesses, let us throw off everything that hinders and the sin that so easily entangles, and let us run with perseverance the race marked out for us.*
> Hebrews 12: 1

In the Old Testament, the priests and prophets were God's accountability agents. In the New Testament, the disciples were accountable to Jesus and to one another. As 21st Century disciples, leaders are accountable to Jesus and should be accountable to one another.

Implementation will require accountability. On the front end of the planning process, establish time line of accountability. Determine who is accountable to whom and an accepted mechanism for activating that accountability. In most cases, building a system of mutually agreed upon checks and balances initially will keep them from ever having to be used.

When Do We Make Adjustments To The Plan?

In good plans, opportunities are built in for periodic evaluation and fine-tuning. The rule of thumb is that the more global the level of planning, the less adjustment should be made. Your purpose as a church should nearly never change. As we have stated, in the church our purpose will always be the same unless we hear again from God. <u>We are to make disciples.</u>

- Our vision should be a long-term proposition based on who our church is. Unless there are major changes in our circumstances, our vision should rarely change. (This should even include a change in pastoral leadership. An individual does not need to change the frame on a pair of glasses if they change optometrists!)
- Objectives change as we accomplish the goals that we have established and move on to new possibilities as we fulfill our vision.
- Goals must always be specific, attainable, measurable and desirable.
- Strategies often must be fine-tuned depending on the underlying circumstances of our work.

As we keep our focus on the main target on the horizon, small course adjustments are always necessary. Fine-tuning should be just that. Plans, by and large, should be allowed to run their course. By staying the course, we will win the race.

How Do We Keep The Process Of Master Planning Alive?

As we have said before, the church is a very unusual organism. Leadership and even pastors can change too often. In this environment, it is very difficult to develop a plan that will be sustained for decades rather than just months. How do you build a master plan that will survive not only through the current regime's reign, but also far into the future?

> *The leader should always have dreams he cannot complete and visions that will last far beyond his tenure. Then the mission is more important than the man. Then the people matter even when the next*

leader takes over. Then there is hope and not just history. Leaders who finish well are not those who run the last race before the track lights are turned off. Leaders who finish well are those who pass the baton to their successors to run the next leg of the race. Blessed are those who make their successors succeed.
<u>Leadership That Works</u>, Leith Anderson

The purpose, vision and master plan should be bigger than individuals. Your plan should capture the imagination and commitment of your congregation for generations. Understanding who you are and what you stand for will ignite the fires of your success for years and years and years.

The process is as important as the results. We are to make disciples, which at its fundamental level means we are to learn how to plan and work together.

What Will Be Our Greatest Barrier To Success?

The Surgeon General frequently attaches warnings to products to keep us aware of the possible ramifications of their use. The Food and Drug Administration also spends millions of dollars testing products to discover the consequences resulting from using them on our skin, breathing them, seeing them and having them in the environments. As Christians, we must do the same.

Finally, be strong in the Lord and in His mighty power. Put on the full armor of God so that you can take your stand against the devil's schemes. For our struggle is not against flesh and blood, but against the rulers, against the authorities, against the powers of this dark world and against the spiritual forces of evil in the heavenly realms. Ephesians 6: 10-12

A church on the edge of implementing a divinely inspired plan for changing the world for the Lord Jesus Christ

is a serious and intimidating threat to Satan. You must understand that especially at this stage, he will do everything in his power to keep you from moving forward. Focusing on Jesus Christ will keep the devil at bay.

What Is Our Assurance?

Now to him who is able to do immeasurably more than all we ask or imagine, according to His power that is at work within us, to him be glory in the church and in Christ Jesus throughout all generations, for ever and ever! Amen. Ephesians 3: 20-21

What is our assurance that we can and will be successful as we seek to be more effective leaders and a more effective church? God wants us to be! He wants to bless us with His power so that we might have an extraordinary impact on the world.

Having completed this study on the Ten Components of the Effective Church, you have been exposed to an architecture designed to be a model for your church to emulate so that you can be effective in your service to the Lord. It is not as much a list of *things to do to be effective*, as it is a working environment within which to operate. As you stay aware of these Ten Components and strive to employ them in your church, you will be more successful for the Lord.

For this architecture to be helpful, its underlying premise must adhere to the spiritual. There must be a foundational assumption embraced that God loves you. He loves your church. He has developed a plan for your church. He has provided you with all of the tools necessary to accomplish that plan for Him. The church's job is to discover the plan, develop the gifts and deploy its members to service – and trust in God.

Action Steps:
1. Honestly, it is not difficult to gather a consensus in a church that changes need to be made. However, taking the initiative to implement these changes can be difficult. Consider the following questions individually and corporately.

    a. Where is this church in the planning process?

    _____
    _____
    _____

    b. Is this church serious about discerning God's plan for the church?

    _____
    _____
    _____

    c. What do you need to do next to begin action?

    _____
    _____
    _____

2. Prayer is the ultimate key to success. Spend time in individual and corporate prayer over the Ten Components. Intentionally build a vital and healthy atmosphere of prayer surrounding these efforts. Remember to keep your prayer chain updated on the praises!

3. Consider the Process of Renewal. How can your church be more intentional about energizing and renewing your church by planning events periodically to enhance your ministry?

    _____
    _____
    _____

LRM is committed to serving the local church as it renews, motivates and equips men and women for ministry. We believe that renewal is a process. As churches commit themselves to consistent and intentional levels of:

- Leadership Renewal and Development
- Congregational Renewal
- Mission, Vision and Strategy
- Resourcing and Equipping

the church will experience healthy ministry and vital growth.

One More Chapter?

Wait a minute! Don't they teach in seminary that when you finish a message, you should be finished? End it! Don't keep going!

Sorry, but we have one more short chapter. Why? As the church has been studied throughout history, it has become clear that churches have vision and life cycles. When a church is new (or renewed), the members and visitors alike can sense and see the "dancing on the line." Simply defined, dancing on the line results from the efforts of the church to reach out to those immersed in spiritual chaos. Focused on self, the people in this realm are headed to eternal death in hell. The church is doing everything in its power to reach out to these people who are being called by God and bring them over the line into the realm of spiritual order.

In this area, the Holy Spirit effects life change in the hearts of these individuals. Vital growth occurs in the life of the church. This growth may occur numerically, but it definitely will occur spiritually. To assist with this growth, the church will develop organizational structures (which STILL are a good thing!). However, with these structures can (not will, but can) come a blockage called "THE RUT."

With this blockage, the Holy Spirit is unintentionally pushed aside as man becomes the primary agent in the church. Motivational death occurs, as programs become the focus over ministry. Programs are not bad things, but when they become institutionalized, ministry is lost. Creativity and excitement are lost until vision is renewed.

Renewed vision is the key. As we discussed in the introduction to the last chapter, Peter experienced a renewed vision as the risen Christ called him back to feed his sheep. Peter's three denials were literally erased as Jesus called him back three times. "The Rock" was restored in his relationship and affirmed in his ability to lead.

What is the first thing most campers do after they wake up on a cold morning? Stir the ashes and rebuild the fire. Our churches need to have a time in which we can call back the "drifting sheep" to a renewed focus of serving God. This is not a trivial time to simply throw together. This is a passionate time to stoke the fire and encourage the walk.

It hurts to step on a nail. I've related my experience to you of working on the construction site. Honestly, that was nothing.

Two thousand years ago, our Savior had nails driven into His flesh.

His hands and feet were pierced.

His blood was poured out on the ground.

He did that for me.

He did that for you.

Those very same nails that were used to kill our King should be used to drive you to build a church that will glorify Him in all that is done. How is your fire today? Do you need the ashes stirred in your heart so that you can break out of your rut and serve the King anew?

This is important.

Don't waste time.

Don't make excuses.

Just do it.

There is no Plan B.

Accept it.

Work with it.

Thank God for it.

For this reason I kneel before the Father, from whom His whole family in heaven and on earth derives its name. I pray that out of His glorious riches He may strengthen you with power through His Spirit in your inner being, so that Christ may dwell in your hearts through faith. And I pray that you, being rooted and established in love, may have power, together with all the saints, to grasp how wide and long and high and deep is the love of Christ, and to know this love that surpasses knowledge – that you may be filled to the measure of the fullness of God.

Ephesians 3: 14-19